Praise for *The Good, the Bad, and Your Business: Choosing Right When Ethical Dilemmas Pull You Apart*

"Jeff Seglin is one of the most thoughtful writers on business ethics today. Well-written and lucid, this book does not preach; it teaches the reader how to think intelligently about hard choices. Every executive who wants to build a successful business—and wants to do so with integrity—should read this book."

—Jim Collins, coauthor *Built to Last*

"For any business person dealing with money, people, or society, *The Good, the Bad, and Your Business* should be required reading."

—Jim McCann, CEO, 1-800-FLOWERS.COM

"*The Good, the Bad, and Your Business* demonstrates what we have always believed—that we do well in business only when we are also doing good."

—Jeffrey B. Swartz, president and CEO, Timberland

"It's a rare business book that can truly change your life, and Jeff Seglin's latest is just that. You'll find no grandstanding or buzzwords, but rather a compelling blend of research and worldly experience, written by a master. He's the perfect travel guide for the examined life we all must lead to achieve meaningful success. Don't miss this one!"

—Steven Leveen, cofounder and president, Levenger

"Just when you thought all the angles on management had been tackled, along comes *The Good, the Bad, and Your Business*. This is the first book to address everyday business ethics and their powerful potential for disaster or triumph. Shaped as much by Seglin's expertise as by business readers' responses to his "Black and White" column in *Inc.*, this book will change the way you make business decisions."

—George Gendron, editor-in-chief, *Inc.* magazine

"The human imagination has always been challenged and moved through compelling stories. Jeffrey Seglin's book is brimming with real stories, provocative dilemmas, and authentic perspectives."

—Pierre Ferrari, board member, Ben & Jerry's Homemade, Inc.

"Jeff Seglin has written a book that will instantly be the standard against which all discussions of ethics in the workplace will be compared. With the skill of a neurosurgeon and the studied neutrality of a Freudian psychoanalyst, Seglin guides readers to a spot squarely between the horns of those ethical dilemmas that are of greatest concern to business people and does just what he should. . . . let's you sit there and struggle with the evidence and analysis by yourself. Amazingly, Seglin never moralizes, sermonizes, or imposes any judgmental guidance. Instead, he has created a page turner on a subject with a well deserved reputation for demagoguery and pedantry. No professional who has—or longs for—a conscience can ignore this book."

—Dr. Steven Berglas, lecturer, Harvard Medical School,
Instructor, Anderson School of Management, UCLA,
and *Inc.* columnist

"*The Good, the Bad, and Your Business* offers us something rarely found in business ethics: a presentation that pulls the reader into the *reality* of managerial decision-making. It is a world where ethics counts for everything but the ethical trigger points are entangled in people issues, time pressures, financial urgency and simple avoidance of uncomfortable choices. Seglin's informed and sensitive treatment leads us through these obstacles toward a path of open dialogue and honest questioning. In an increasingly complex and networked business culture, such road maps to ethics are a navigational must."

—Laura Nash, director, Institute for
Values-Centered Leadership, Harvard Divinity School

"Finally—a book about modern ethics and business that you don't have to get all dressed up to read! Writing with a sure touch, lively language and a wonderful wit that, until now, have been depressingly absent from all those dreary ethics debates, Jeff Seglin has found a way to wake up his subject without once getting bogged down. He never lectures, finger-points, gets cute, or drones on, and in the process he's built something entirely fresh and new: he knows his stuff and he respects his readers' intelligence. This terrific book is the next best thing to talking to your smart, warm, and funny best friend about the toughest decisions you'll ever have to make. **It's flat-out superb.**"

—Nancy K. Austin, coauthor, *A Passion For Excellence*

"Like his *New York Times* column, Jeff Seglin doesn't sugar coat the subject of business ethics. *The Good, the Bad, and Your Business* gives us a clear roadmap through the treacherous terrain of what's right, what's wrong. It's a terrific book."

—Pierre Mornell, author of *Hiring Smart*

"Seglin's provocative book shows that our choices and actions give evidence of what we stand for. And that is the real bottom line in business and in life."

—Daniel A. Phillips, president, Fiduciary Trust (Boston)

"This book will open your eyes to the importance of those seemingly insignificant business decisions you make every day. You'll sleep better having read *The Good, the Bad, and Your Business*."

—Andy Smith, comanager, Harley-Davidson University

"Jeffrey Seglin has unparalleled insights into how to wrestle with everyday dilemmas in our pressure-cooker business environments. He offers sound advice on how to translate our values into actions so we can navigate our way through the complex situations we face daily."

—Carol Raphael, president and CEO,
Visiting Nurse Service of New York

"Seglin has written a 'feet on the ground' practical walk through the kind of ethical challenges that are a part of day-to-day business. Whether the issues are cash flow, personnel, or public disclosure, this is a great read for managers who want to do "the right thing"—which is rarely obvious and usually complex."

—Sharon Daloz Parks, coauthor, *Common Fire:
Leading Lives of Commitment in a Complex World*

the good, the bad, and your business

choosing right when ethical dilemmas pull you apart

Jeffrey L. Seglin

Foreword by Norman R. Augustine

JOHN WILEY & SONS, INC.

New York • Chichester • Weinheim • Brisbane • Singapore • Toronto

To Evan, for Mondays,
and Nancy, for always

Copyright © 2000 by Jeffrey L. Seglin. All rights reserved.

Published by John Wiley & Sons, Inc.
Published simultaneously in Canada.

Some parts of this book appeared originally in different form in *Inc.* magazine. Specifically, these include the "Black and White" columns which appeared in the January, April, July, and the special *Inc.* 500 issues in 1998 as well as the February and May issues of 1999. The specific use of these articles is indicated in the footnotes. Reprinted with permission, *Inc.* magazine. Copyright 1998 and 1999 by Goldhirsh Group, Inc., 38 Commercial Wharf, Boston, MA 02110.

This publication is designed to provide accurate and authoritative information in regard to the subject matter covered. It is sold with the understanding that the publisher is not engaged in rendering professional services. If legal, accounting, medical, psychological or any other expert assistance is required, the services of a competent professional person should be sought.

Library of Congress Cataloging-in-Publication Data:

Seglin, Jeffrey L., 1956–
    The good, the bad, and your business : choosing right when ethical dilemmas pull you apart / Jeffrey L. Seglin.
      p. cm.
    Includes bibliographical references and index.
    ISBN 0-471-34779-5 (alk. paper)
    1. Business ethics. 2. Decision making—Moral and ethical aspects. I. Title.
HF5387.S426   2000
658.4′03—dc21   99-059986

Printed in the United States of America.

10 9 8 7 6 5 4 3 2 1

Contents

Foreword

One segment of the course I have been teaching at Princeton addresses ethics in business . . . some in the general public would say an oxymoron . . . but not I.

As a part of that topic, the students confront a case study involving the Greenacres Lawnmower Company, a firm that has just been notified by the police that seven persons have died after being struck by blades flying off rotary mowers produced by Greenacres. Further investigation indicates that someone has intentionally weakened the blades involved in the incidents—almost certainly after the lawnmowers left the factory. A debate breaks out within the company's management whether all the lawnmowers previously sold by the firm should be recalled for inspection and whether a major advertising campaign should be initiated to warn consumers of the potential hazard of using one of Greenacres' most important products.

From a legal standpoint, the argument is made that the company almost certainly has no direct responsibility for the problem. Greenacres has a responsibility to its shareholders not to destroy their investments through an overreaction to a situation not of the company's creation. From a customer satisfaction and safety standpoint, it is argued that the advertising campaign and product recall effort should commence immediately to warn all users of the potential danger posed by Greenacres' lawnmowers. Somewhat surprisingly, from the standpoint of the police, a highly publicized recall campaign might cause what is thus-far a relatively confined, albeit serious, problem to expand into other areas by encouraging copy-cat crimes. And from a public relations standpoint, the choice seems merely to be a matter of selecting which type of disaster the company's management prefers.

As the students discuss how they would handle the dilemma if they happened to be Greenacres' CEO, a stranger sits quietly in the back of the classroom listening intently. When the students have finished presenting their solutions, the stranger is introduced. He is Jim Burke, the CEO of Johnson & Johnson at the time that company faced a very similar set of facts in the Tylenol™ tampering murders some years earlier. A robust debate invariably breaks out among the students.

In dealing with ethics, it is generally easy to conclude after the fact what should have been done since the outcome of the course actually chosen is known. This is why I disguise the Johnson & Johnson case, as well as the other cases we study, and why I often invite a guest participant who has had real-world experience in dealing with the issue at hand.

Somewhat to my surprise, when the course is rated by the students at the end of the semester, one of the segments that they invariably would liked to have had the opportunity to treat further was the one concerning ethics.

Similarly, in my prior life as CEO of the Lockheed Martin Corporation, where every one of our nearly 200,000 employees, starting with myself, underwent ethics awareness training every year, the experience turned out to be universally fascinating and welcome. Those who began the sessions as skeptics often became the most enthusiastic and involved participants in the discussions that ensued.

But this should be expected, since ethics represents the very bedrock of business. It is this truism that causes Jeff Seglin's book to be such important and fascinating reading . . . helped greatly by his nonpreachy style.

There seems to be four underlying problems that dominate attempts to achieve ethical comportment in business. The first is recognizing that an ethical issue is in fact being confronted. This is why the course I taught at Princeton and why Lockheed Martin's ethics program focus on ethical awareness. Most people who get themselves—and their companies—into serious ethical trouble are decent people: they just make one colossal mistake . . . usually because they don't stop to think until it is too late.

The second problem in achieving ethical comportment is figuring out what is in fact the right thing to do. This goes far beyond merely complying with the law. The late Supreme Court Justice Potter Stewart once defined ethics as "knowing the difference between what you have a right to do, and what is the right thing to do." Some people believe that if it's legal, it's ethical. Justice Stewart obviously didn't agree with that. Neither do I.

The third problem is perhaps the most common: knowing what is the right thing to do and not having the fortitude to do it.

And, finally, the fourth challenge in embracing ethical behavior is that doing the right thing does not always guarantee a "good" outcome . . . in the short-term. On the other hand, I am absolutely convinced that ethical behavior by both individuals and businesses does pay off in the long-term—in both the pragmatic as well as the philosophical sense.

Today there seems to be an explosion of interest in ethics in the business and business-school community . . . and apparently not a minute too soon, either. Public confidence surveys invariably show business (the surveys generally make a bad situation worse when they bias the answers by using the descriptor, "Big Business" in their questionnaires) enjoying little public respect—ranking right in there with politicians, the media, and axe murderers.

Recent cases of insider trading, industrial espionage, perfuming IPOs, managing profits, "cooking" the books, bribing foreign officials, and more, have taken their toll. But, as can be seen from Seglin's book, such behavior need not be accepted.

Borrowing from my own experience in the last decade, I had the occasion to participate in putting together five different multibillion dollar mergers and acquisitions. Each was sealed with a handshake and in each case that act proved far more binding than all the legalese the lawyers were able to conjure. The CEOs involved in these deals were people of the stature of Jack Welch of General Electric, Dan Tellep of Lockheed, Bill Anders and Jim Mellor of General Dynamics, Bernard Schwartz of Loral, and Kent Kressa of Northrop Grumman. My policy is simple: Deal only with people you can trust . . . life is too short to do otherwise.

America's greatest investor, Warren Buffett, once advised his son, "It takes twenty years to build a reputation and five minutes to ruin it. If you think about that you'll do things differently." And Henry David Thoreau once observed, "Goodness is the only investment that never fails." In this book, Jeff Seglin builds a strong case why both are correct . . . as well as how to avoid the four pitfalls to building a truly ethical and highly successful organization.

NORMAN R. AUGUSTINE
Chairman of the Executive Committee
Lockheed Martin Corporation
Bethesda, Maryland

Acknowledgments

The idea for a book on how people in business face ethical dilemmas came from a variety of sources. I'd always been fascinated by the subject, but it wasn't until I started writing about it and receiving the reader feedback that I began to believe there was something about the subject that got readers thinking and reacting in ways that were far more insightful, personal, and passionate than they had to other subjects I'd written about in business.

Many readers wrote reacting to cases I'd written and told me about their own experiences as well as the challenges they faced in their businesses. Others wrote asking for help or for ideas about who could help them as they faced dilemmas they found overwhelming. Still others wrote to offer ideas or cheer on the subject. Oh sure, there were several readers who wrote to tell me I was way off or that I would surely be lambasted for a stance I'd taken, but they too were helpful in letting me know what issues readers found relevant as well as provocative. This book couldn't have been written without the feedback and ideas from all of those readers.

I've been particularly blessed while writing this book to have been a resident Fellow at the Center for the Study of Values in Public Life at Harvard University. This fellowship, funded in part by a grant from the Lilly Foundation, gave me access to the vast resources at Harvard as well as a wonderfully diverse community to tap into for guidance and insight. Specifically at the Center, Brent Coffin, Laura Nash, Donna Verschueren, and Missy Daniel offered constant support. My fellow Fellows—Linda Nicholson, Janet Jakobsen, Jon Gunnemann, and Jim Wallis—responded to some early drafts of chapters and leant support throughout the year. Jim Carroll, Joe Badaracco, John Case, and Loren Gary were also tremendously supportive in their reading of some of the manuscript.

Nancy Nienhuis, the program coordinator for the Center, managed to coordinate the seminar I lead that drew together a regular cadre of graduate students from both the Harvard Divinity and Harvard Business schools through the entire academic year. She also attended each session and joined in as the students reacted to various parts of this book. These student discussions had a tremendous influence on my writing. Of particular help was John Morse's valuable feedback and work in virtue ethics. And Lia Holden, who worked as my research assistant throughout the year, simultaneously assisted and challenged my ideas and the material is the better for it.

Many colleagues read pieces of the manuscript at various stages and offered advice. Particularly helpful were Tom Richman, Leslie Brokaw, Nancy Austin, and Jim Lewis, who kept asking for more chapter drafts to see who would win in the end.

The ideas that are included in the book came from many sources, but of particular help in finding good ideas and thinking them through were Steve Berglas, John Waggoner, Pierre Mornell, Mark McIntyre, Cornelia Lewine, Mike Hofman, and Norman Brodsky. Robert Bertsche and Kascha Piotrzkowski have my undying gratitude for holding my feet to the fire when it came to checking and double-checking facts and source materials.

I'm grateful to Lexis-Nexis which provided web research assistance to this project by providing access to its online Lexis-Nexis Universe product.

I've written about business ethics for *Inc.* magazine and the Sunday *New York Times*. Without question, my editors at both publications helped me in ways for which I can't begin to thank them. First and foremost they challenged me to think through and to articulate the dilemmas I was writing about as clearly as possible so that readers would get the point of what I was writing. While they weren't involved in the writing of this book, my relationships with Jim Schachter and Patrick Lyons at *The New York Times* have shaped the way I think about the material here. At *Inc.*, Josh Hyatt acted more as a collaborator than an editor on many of the business ethics pieces that have been adapted with permission in various parts of this book. Whether he agreed with my point or not, Josh always pushed me to find a way to articulate clearly without losing my own sense of what the real issues in the pieces were. It was after a discussion with George Gendron at *Inc.* that I first started writing about various aspects of business ethics. I am grateful to him for the opportunity as well as his patience and support as we've tried to find a way of writing about this topic that is neither preachy nor naïve, but instead captures the attention of seasoned businesspeople who regularly grapple with tough business dilemmas. Josh, George, and the rest of my colleagues at *Inc.* provided great support throughout this project.

I'm also grateful to my agent, Jonathon Lazear, as well as his colleague Christi Cardenas. It was Jonathon who sold the idea for this book based on the work I was planning to do during my fellowship year at Harvard. Throughout the year, he and Christi have been tremendously supportive. So too has Renana Meyers, my editor at John Wiley & Sons. From the outset, she has been committed to the project. Her feedback on each chapter as I finished it was invaluable. She forced me to think hard and write clearly, but did so with incredible grace and support.

My family has done far more than tolerate my absences or preoccupations throughout the year. My father, Lester, called regularly offering support and encouragement. My children, Bethany, David, Ed, and Lisa have engaged me regularly in discussions about material in the book and offered not only support but also ideas and guidance. My grandson, Evan, who was born while I was writing this book, kept 'me company on Mondays and made my life fuller in every way. My wife, Nancy, a former book editor and now a child psychologist, has put both vocations to work in seeing me through this project. She read every word in the first draft of this book as it was being written. Her input, support, and compassion as this book was being written go a long way toward explaining why she is the woman I'd eat bees for.

JEFFREY L. SEGLIN
jseglin@post.harvard.edu

1

It Hurts so Good

W hen a good friend who is a fairly high-profile literary agent heard that I had decided to take a year's leave to write a book on the language of business in ethics, he sent me a short note: "Good for you," he wrote. "But let me warn you, my friend, that using the word 'ethics' in the title of a book is the kiss of death."

He wasn't the first to caution me that the vast reading public, and particularly those in the business world—which I'd been covering for the past 15 years as an editor and writer—were either turned off or scared off by the word *ethics* when it was used in articles or books for business owners and managers. Perhaps the word suggested too moralistic a tone or that a whole lot of judging would be going on.

But this reticence flew in the face of what I'd been experiencing since I had started to write a regular column on business ethics for *Inc.* magazine in late 1997. We'd noticed that every time we ran a story in the magazine about a company or person whose behavior teetered on the brink of outlandishly questionable ethics, we were deluged with letters. And we'd get the letters in waves. The first wave of letters would take us to task for profiling the exploits of a businessperson who perhaps appeared to practice less-than above-board tactics in dealing with his customers, vendors, or employees. After we'd publish some of those letters in the magazine, we'd get a second wave of letters taking the first-wave writers to task for being so judgmental and failing to recognize that in business you face many pressures that force you to make decisions that might give the appearance of being questionable.

On one such occasion, in September 1996, Ed Welles, a senior writer at *Inc.*, wrote about Eyal Balle and his Los Angeles-based shoe company, Rebels.[1] In the article, titled "Basic Instincts," Welles wrote about Balle having "the knack" when it came to selling and building his company. Readers took issue with the fact that Balle had sold himself to Israeli manufacturers as the representative of a big corporate buyer in the United States, which he wasn't. Many readers also cringed when Welles recounted the story of how, when the business was first getting started, Balle had bought a used car for $500, told a friend he'd paid $1,000 for it, and sold it to the friend for $750. The magazine received more letters about this piece than it does about most articles. The vast majority of the letters scolded Balle for practicing such unethical behavior and the magazine for championing him as someone with a knack that was worthy of emulation. "All I know is you have to be creative," Balle had told Welles. "You have no choice but to keep maneuvering." Many readers felt strongly that Balle's maneuvering had crossed the line separating right behavior from wrong.

In a boxed paragraph that accompanied the letters, I wrote about how taken aback we were by the sheer volume of response to this article. And I wondered whether readers drew a distinction between Balle's behavior and other standard business practices that stretched the truth or at the very least maneuvered around it. Was it any different, I asked, than companies that recast their earnings projections when putting together a business plan they were going to shop around to prospective investors for their business?

The next wave of letters began to pour in as soon as the magazine issue with that box and the reader's letters from the first wave hit the stands. This second wave of letter writers took issue with the letter writers who'd judged Balle so harshly. He was just a smart guy trying to get his fledgling business off the ground with very little in the way of financial resources, they wrote.

But there was also another group of readers who wrote in to tell me what a bonehead I'd been to make such an absurd observation as the one I'd made about recasting projections in a business plan. How could I draw a correlation between this and misrepresenting yourself to a manufacturer, they wondered? Creating a business plan with various scenarios was standard operating procedure when trying to get off the ground. Lying to your friend about what you'd paid for a used car you were about to sell him was a wholly different matter.

I knew we'd hit a nerve. While there was no clear right or wrong answer here, readers had strong feelings on both sides of the issue.

Since my first column on business ethics appeared about the compromises a CEO made as he struggled to make payroll, it's become clear from the reporting and the response that businesspeople struggle with ethical decision making day in and day out. More often than not, they talk and think about these issues "obliquely." There seems to be no comfortable language for them to talk about ethics. Even what constitutes an "ethical issue" is unclear to many in business.

Common Misperceptions about Ethics in Business

One of the things that has struck me the most since carving out this beat has been how common it is for people in business to think of a decision as being ethical only if it ended up having dire consequences on the business. Rather than think of ethics as the benchmark against which behavior is measured, for many people ethics has come to be equated with something that inflicts pain on a company or requires some hefty sacrifice.

Take the example of the prominent business school which, not long ago, was given several million dollars to rethink how it taught ethics.[2] The school was renowned for its use of case studies to teach business methods. Seeing an opportunity to use this same approach to bring ethical decision making in business alive, the academic team decided to use the case of Johnson & Johnson which, in 1982, recalled 31 million bottles of Tylenol from store shelves after eight people in the United States had died from cyanide-laced capsules.

The case was compelling. That recall cost Johnson & Johnson $240 million and cut its profit on $5 billion in revenues that year by almost 50 percent. The tampering was not the company's fault, but nevertheless it decided to act before it had complete information on what had happened. The product containers were redesigned and new tamperproof packaging was introduced.[3]

Johnson & Johnson's immediate response to the problem saved the Tylenol brand and won the company rave reviews for coming clean and taking immediate action. Ironically, the move turned out to be a huge marketing coup for the company that resulted in significant goodwill from customers.

When a class of MBA students was asked to comment on the ethics of the case, more than one student responded by saying that the case wasn't an example of ethical decision making at all—because the company benefited from the whole affair. It turned out to be a great marketing move for the company, they said. Where was the ethical problem?

Clearly, the students believed that without pain and suffering, the example ceased to be a case of ethics. Their thinking may have been off-base, but it's not all that uncommon. That pain must ensue from ethical decision making is a commonly held notion. Forget that the leaders at Johnson & Johnson had to make some pretty wrenching decisions and react quickly to a devastating situation. Forget that they weighed their decision knowing that eight people had died and that others were potentially vulnerable.

These life-and-death issues threw the company into making decisions that forced them to weigh right and wrong. And it caused the executives to arrive at a solution that they felt would stem the tide of remarkably devastating circumstances. Regardless of the fact that the public reacted positively to the company's actions and it gained a lot of good will, the company's decision was, in every sense of the word, ethical.

Don't get me wrong, making tough decisions like the one the leaders at Johnson & Johnson made can be painful and gut-wrenching. But—and it's a big but here—they don't have to end with pain and suffering to be considered ethical decisions.

What the students in the MBA class failed to recognize was that on a daily basis, we all make ethical decisions. Sometimes it's as simple as deciding whether or not to credit a coworker with an idea that originated with her that you've brought up in a meeting. Other times it may be deciding just how much information you disclose to colleagues about an office rumor making the rounds. The results of such decisions rarely have the magnitude of the Tylenol case, but they are ethical decisions nonetheless. Based on what you know of the acceptable behavior of the group you belong to, you're trying to decide on the right thing to do.

This notion of "acceptable behavior of the group" is an important one. When it comes to right and wrong, it's important to examine decisions in the context of the culture you're in. Johnson & Johnson, for example, for years has had a strong corporate credo in place that has guided the management in the company during day-to-day operations as well as in times of crisis. Having a clear understanding of your company's culture is key to understanding what "acceptable behavior" is. "Although Johnson & Johnson has periodically reviewed and slightly revised the wording of the credo since 1943," write

Jim Collins and Jerry Porras in *Built to Last: Successful Habits of Visionary Companies,* "the essential ideology—the hierarchy of responsibilities descending from customers down to shareholders and the explicit emphasis on *fair* return rather than maximum return—has remained consistent throughout the history of the credo."[4]

NAVIGATING DILEMMAS DAY-TO-DAY

I don't know where the perception that ethics equals pain came from. In fact, if you think about it, the argument could be made that sorting out ethical dilemmas is actually a search for comfort. We're struggling to find a place where we can be comfortable with our decisions. We're trying to figure out the code that drives human behavior in our society, or in a more narrow sense, our business dealings.

The etymology of the word *ethics* is simple enough. It derives from the Greek term *ethos* (which we carry over into English with at least a similar meaning). One of the modern definitions of ethos is *accustomed place.* In the New Testament, ethos was used in the more or less classic sense of a *home place.* It was the place of safety, where humans and animals alike could gather at the end of the day and be protected.[5] By extension, it came to be used as a description of the norms of behavior that provided a comparable protection to the coherence of a society. So ethical decisions can be said to be decisions that insure the safety of a society's sense of order and justice.

The perplexing part is that trying to determine what falls into that sense of order and justice can be difficult. The range between right and wrong can be vast. We generally recognize—or at least we hope we do—when we're operating at the margins. We can tell when we're going well beyond what's expected in the way of right behavior. And we also know when we've decided that something that falls squarely into the category of questionable or wrong behavior. What we struggle with every day is operating in between the extremes. How completely right do we really *need* to be in our behavior?

In business, the pressures are magnified, because business owners and managers are faced with competing demands to keep a company going. Does the need to make a profit outweigh the need to reward our employees fairly? Does making payroll count more than paying vendors? Do we cut corners on manufacturing processes to keep costs down when our shortcuts might result in unsafe or polluting outcomes? Does our commitment to an employee in trouble outweigh the financial burden he places on the company?

You get the picture. Navigating through the relentless dilemmas that face businesspeople is a day-to-day, moment-to-moment process. So if we deal with such dilemmas all the time, why is it so hard to talk about them?

One reason it's so hard is that when we broach the subject, the discussion often sways into language that sounds judgmental at best and strident at worst. Moral overtones can turn into religious didacticism—or simply perceived that way. We hear talk of the need to have "moral imperatives" in business and society and while few of us would argue the merits of the notion, the speaker of the words often comes off sounding like he is passing judgment on anyone and everyone who doesn't buy into his concept of morality.

What's more, unless you're listening to a preacher give a sermon, the moment someone opens his mouth and words like *moral* or *ethical* come out, more often than not the listener shuts down or wonders *who this speaker thinks he is* to sit in judgment on everyone else. The traditional words used to talk about ethics and morality when applied to the dilemmas we face in business are charged. Rather than enabling us to have a meaningful discussion about actions we might take, we're instead put on guard. We become indecisive, lest we be judged to somehow be lacking in moral rectitude.

And, as any seasoned business manager knows, indecision can be the kiss of death in a highly competitive, fast-moving economy. While you're wracking over the appropriate behavior and how to talk about it, your competitor could be passing you by, nibbling at market share and perhaps a hefty portion of your gross profits along with it.

When your employees sense indecision and aren't clear on the direction the company is taking, productivity can drop off. When that happens, kiss employee morale goodbye. Not having the words to talk about these complex issues can do more than catch us off guard. It can also take a hefty helping out of our company's bottom line.

WHEN WORDS FAIL US

An added complication is that when we talk about ethical behavior in business, too frequently we're really talking about what kind of behavior people in business need to assume to avoid litigation. We put behavior policies in place so we don't get sued for sexual harassment, penalizing minority workers, slandering poor-performing employees. With workplace litigation exploding over the past several years (more than 24,000 wrongful termination suits were filed in 1997 alone, up from 10,000 in 1990[6]), our actions too often are driven by doing what we have to do to keep a cap on legal costs rather than doing what we really believe is the right thing to do. When this happens, we relegate many ethical decisions to the human resources or legal departments. And when we stop thinking about this stuff for ourselves, it's no wonder we don't know the words to use when we do discuss it.

When sophisticated businesspeople try to talk deliberately about ethics, words often become an issue. Though fluent in cost-benefit analyses and accrual accounting methods, when it comes time to articulate thoughts on what constitutes ethical behavior, they use words like, *honor, true,* and *duty.* The lack of language to talk about ethical behavior in business stems in part from the fact that the last time these businesspeople discussed issues like this was when they were in the Boy Scouts. Words directly from the Boy Scout code of honor? It's another sign that when it comes to talking about ethics in the workplace, our vocabulary is limited to touchstones from our youth, ones that may no longer feel comfortable. We need a fresh way to talk about the dilemmas we face.

So, Why This Book?

Well, for one thing, this book is an attempt to draw a distinction between behavior based on a fear of litigation versus behavior driven by ethics. But this book is also an attempt to show how most of us do or avoid doing ethical decision making almost every day in business. We're faced with decisions of varying degrees of importance that force us to choose how we're going to respond, behave, or react, knowing fully that we're making tradeoffs, judgments, and close calls on a regular basis. We may not come up with the same decisions or actions as the manager or owner next to us would have, but we make the decisions nonetheless.

While we all face ethical decisions every day, we're often unable to act in a way that resolves them. The trouble is that often we don't know how to articulate what the actual dilemma is and as a result we find it difficult to formulate clear possible solutions. When it comes to speaking clearly about ethical dilemmas, words fail us.

The premise of this book is that in business, we're all searching for a comfortable way to navigate these decisions. By *comfortable,* I don't mean complacent. Business is a dynamic, fast-paced thing and we can hardly stand idly by hoping that the answers to our dilemmas will be revealed to us in a puff of smoke or a revelatory strike. That's why trying to come to an understanding of how to talk about ethics in a meaningful way is so critical to the operation of a business. We need to be able to understand the context we're operating in and to make decisions fully informed with a clear sense of right and wrong, so we can weigh out the tough decisions we need to make to stay honed for competition.

The *comfort* we're looking for is that place where we can continue to stay a lean, mean, profit machine, but at the same time do it with an understanding of *what we stand for in the way we make choices and decisions.* Contrary to some popular thinking, being ethical in business and generating profits do not need to be mutually exclusive actions.

Think of this book then as a search for a comfort level among the conflicting spheres of business you operate in. While there are overlaps in these spheres, I've divided the exploration into three areas of business that we all commonly deal with. The first is money, the second is people, and the third is the common good, which includes all of those areas that we don't traditionally think of as part of the economic bottom-line business function, but which we have to factor into our decision making all the time. How do you manage all of these issues in the context of how you run or do your business?

The money and people aspects of managing a business are pretty obvious—they are the critical ingredients to all successful businesses. While we need to make them on a regular basis, these decisions are often loaded with moral ambiguity, packed with the stuff about which ethical decisions are made.

The first part—the money chapters—will look at the difficult decisions company owners and managers must make when faced with trying to keep cash flow strong enough to keep a company running. Shortages of cash can make the most honest of us consider behavior we never would have anticipated.

The second part—the people chapters—look at how we deal with issues directly involving people in the workplace, whether it be deciding how far to go to help a troubled employee, what stance if any to have on romantic relationships between coworkers, how and what to communicate to the rest of the workforce when an employee is fired, and how employees pass between personal and business lives when the line grows constantly blurrier.

The third part—the common good chapters—include such things as where we draw the line between posturing and lying, if and how we legitimize spying on competitors, and how our operations affect the environment.

Obviously, our dealings with these three spheres are not so cleanly segregated in our day-to-day business lives. They overlap—decisions we make about money often involve people and those we make about issues relating to the common good frequently touch on the other two as well. What comforts us in one area may not do so in another.

It would be nice and clean if we could think of the three areas as interlocking circles—as in a classic Venn diagram. And it would be neater still if we could say that the area of comfort we're searching for is that small area where all three circles overlap. But alas, it's just not that simple. Finding that comfort level is finding a spot that shifts and mutates moment to moment, decision to decision.

Remember: Comfort does not equal complacency. Nor does the search for it translate into poor performance. John Elkington, in his book *Cannibals with Forks* talks about the need for a triple bottom line in business. Rather than just focus on the economic bottom line, Elkington argues that a company should pay heed to three bottom lines: economic, environmental, and social (or human).[7] Each has its own form of capital and each, Elkington argues, is important for a company that wants to perform well on all levels and to sustain itself into the future. The three spheres in *The Good, the Bad, and Your Business*—money, people, and the common good—are not too dissimilar from Elkington's, although I expand the environmental area to include not just environmental issues but other issues that involve the community in which a particular business operates.

If you buy into the argument that the only responsibility of a business is to its stockholders and that paying attention to areas outside of this will result in a lesser-performing company, the research of two Harvard Business School professors suggests just the opposite. John Kotter and James Heskett studied the performance of 207 large firms over an 11-year period. They wrote of their findings:

Corporate culture can have a significant impact on a firm's long-term economic performance. We found that firms with cultures that emphasized all the key managerial constituencies (customers, stockholders, and employees) and leadership from managers at all levels outperformed firms that did not have those cultural traits by a huge margin. Over an eleven-year period, the former increased revenues

by an average of 682 percent versus 166 percent for the latter, ex-
panded their work forces by 282 percent versus 36 percent, grew
their stock prices by 901 percent versus 74 percent, and improved
their net incomes by 756 percent versus 1 percent.[8]

Consider that final finding again: The companies that paid attention equally to customers, stockholders, and employees outperformed
those that didn't in growth of net income over the 11-year period by
a factor of 756. Paying attention to more than just returning profits
to stockholders can have a huge payoff.

We know how to measure the numbers when it comes to financial performance. But what too often gets in the way of meeting the
needs of all the constituencies of a business—the customers, employees, vendors, community, as well as the investors—is that we have a
difficult time articulating the dilemmas we're thrust into when we
try to balance all of their needs.

The goal of *The Good, the Bad, and Your Business* isn't to teach
you new words or abstractions, adding even more to the stewpot that's
already full to the brim. Instead, it's to use real-life business dilemmas
as a way to help you see how ethical decisions are made and the impact these decisions have on you, your business, and all of its constituencies.

The challenge is to search for that comfort, that ethos, in which
we can operate our businesses knowing that we've made thoughtful
decisions and contemplated the possible impact of the outcomes of
those choices.

But we can't even begin the challenge until we find a way to talk
about making tough choices that somehow has meaning to business
owners—some language that cuts through all the preconceived no-
tions about what it means to be ethical and gets at the heart of the
matter which is, how can we run a business facing all the challenges
and dilemmas we face day-in and day-out and know that we've done
our thoughtful best to do the right thing.

PART ONE

MONEY

I guess it's just a moral or ethical issue for me. When we make a decision to do something, we should be able to explain that decision in the same way to anybody who asks, be it our spouse, our business partner, an employee, a creditor, or a customer. I have to sleep at night.

—Chris Graff
Founder of Marque Inc., a Goshen,
Indiana ambulance manufacturer

The chapters in the first part of *The Good, the Bad, and Your Business* each focus on dilemmas posed by dealing with money issues. Whether it's the strain of struggling to make payroll, deciding if you feel it's right or wrong to use bankruptcy laws to shield you from repaying debts, or choosing just how much you disclose to your accountant when an audit is being done, the events recounted in this chapter begin to form a picture of the complexities of the business world and the choices that must be made in that world on a daily basis.

The intent of these chapters is to help you begin to lay a groundwork that will assist you as you come up against your own dilemmas in the workplace. Clearly, there's no magic template that will tell you how to answer every question or address every challenge as it comes up. But by exploring and analyzing how others have acted, you can begin to get a sense of how to think about your own decisions when faced with dilemmas.

You also come away with a clearer understanding of just how intertwined the decisions you make about money in business are with the people in those business and the community at large. Sure, it's possible to make sound financial decisions without taking into account anything other than the economic bottom line. But in the chapters that follow you can begin to see how failing to take into account the constituencies affected by your financial decisions can very likely have long-term implications to the success of your business.

2

When Payrolls Keep
Us Up at Night

Without question, the issue most responsible for keeping CEOs of new companies up at night is anxiety over making payroll. It's more worrisome than finding good employees, meeting regulatory requirements, or even staying on the good side of the IRS. It's at the start, or when a company hits a growth spurt, that payroll concern becomes all-consuming.

Such is the stuff of great dilemmas in business. When cash is slow to come in and you're facing a stack of bills, where do you allocate the money first? For most startup CEOs, it's the employees they see every day who worry them the most when money's in short supply. There is something about chatting with someone at the watercooler or walking together to the parking lot that makes paying him or her a much more personal commitment than, say, getting payroll taxes off to the Internal Revenue Service or a check to that vendor who dropped off supplies two months ago.

No two people will act exactly the same way when faced with a cash shortage, but money—especially the lack of it—does funny things to people.

But before we explore the dilemma of making payroll, let's first acknowledge that when people need—or at least think they need—money, whether they're CEOs or managers running a business, parents trying to put food on the table, or students trying to pay rent and buy books, that need sometimes forces them to make decisions about their own behavior that they never thought they'd have to make.

In business, it's not just startups or small companies that have to make choices based on issues surrounding access to money. Established public companies with stockholders to answer to often need to show profits and to make tough decisions about what it will take to keep showing those profits. This is as true in flush times as in lean. When the unemployment rate in the United States hit a several-decade low of 4.6 percent in 1998, for example, companies were still cutting a sizable number of employees from the payroll. In January of that year alone, 72,193 jobs were eliminated, up from 58,293 cut in December 1997, and far more than the 43,595 jobs that were cut in January 1997.[1] While it may make sound business sense to reduce employment roles, it still poses a dilemma for companies trying to weigh the needs of stockholders against the needs of employees.

But without question, when a CEO or manager must daily look into the face of the person he might have to layoff, the layoff decision is much harder to make. It's human nature to want to protect someone you know, especially when the person's only shortcoming may be that he happened to join the company more recently than anyone else.

The more impersonal the decision—the more distance the job cutter has from the person being cut from the job—the easier you'd think the decision might be since it's much harder to fire someone when he's sitting in the office next to you. But that's not necessarily the case. Each person will approach the situation with his or her own set of values and concerns. As a result, it's very possible for two people to approach the same dilemma with very different solutions.

DIFFERENT PEOPLE, DIFFERENT CHOICES

There's a well-known case used by Lawrence Kohlberg, a Harvard professor who developed a theory of moral development, that involves a man named Heinz. Heinz has to decide whether to steal a drug that he can't afford but that would save his wife's life. Kohlberg posed Heinz's dilemma to young boys to see where they rated on his scale of moral development.[2] Those boys who said they didn't think Heinz should steal the drug were deemed immature because their responses suggested that they didn't see the situation clearly enough to value a human life over property. One 11-year-old boy named Jake approached the problem as logically as he would a math problem:

> A human life is worth more than money, and if the druggist only makes $1,000, he is still going to live, but if Heinz doesn't steal the drug, his wife is going to die.

When Jake is asked *why* life is worth more than money, the boy responded:

> Because the druggist can get a thousand dollars later from rich people with cancer, but Heinz can't get his wife again.

When asked *why not,* Jake responded:

> Because people are all different and you couldn't get Heinz's wife again.

Fine, you'd think. But when Carol Gilligan, who had studied with Kohlberg posed the same dilemma and question to a group of young girls, the responses were wholly different. When 11-year-old Amy responded to the question, "Should Heinz steal the drug?" she said:

> Well I don't think so. I think there might be other ways besides stealing it, like if he could borrow the money or make a loan or something, but he really shouldn't steal the drug—but his wife shouldn't die either.

When asked why, Amy continued:

> If he stole the drug, he might save his wife then, but if he did, he might have to go to jail, and then his wife might get sicker again, and he couldn't get more of the drug, and it might not be good. So, they should really just talk it out and find some other way to make the money.

"Just as Jake is confident the judge would agree that stealing is the right thing for Heinz to do," wrote Gilligan, "so Amy is confident that, 'if Heinz and the druggist had talked it out long enough, they could reach something besides stealing.' "

Amy saw "a world comprised of relationships" and, unlike Jake, she's baffled at why the druggist wouldn't have automatically responded to the wife's condition.

Gilligan used her study with young girls like Amy to show how Kohlberg's model might be flawed since his sample consisted of young boys who might see the world in a particular way. When Gilligan sampled young girls, they came up with a wholly different set of solutions to the same problem that weren't accounted for on Kohlberg's scale.

The Heinz case is a dramatic example of how gender may play a role in determining the ways different human beings view the world. When I first started reading about how Gilligan's findings called into question Kohlberg's model of moral development, it struck me as a wonderful example of just how differently people can react to, interpret, and deal with the same dilemma.

That's true in business as well. While there are certainly some basic rules you need to follow to be successful in business—such as making more money than you're spending . . . unless of course it's part of your business plan to be unprofitable for a long, long time as is the case with some Internet startups[3]—it's very possible to confront the same dilemma in business and come up with a wholly different solution from the CEO or manager at the company down the street.

In *Ethics in Organizations*, David Murray observes that from "the start it must be emphasized that there can be no rigid, structured method that will automatically give us 'right' answers. We will at many stages be confronted with the need to make judgments. Not everything is quantifiable. Not everything is predictable. We should, however, be able to structure and record our judgments so that our eventual decisions are at the very least explicable, even if not to everyone justifiable."[4]

That's what's at the crux of the matter, isn't it? It's not that we need to have all the right answers. It's that we want to be able to understand and explain (if not to our board, employees, owners, or comanagers, then to ourselves) why we did what we did. We don't want to justify our actions in the sense that we make excuses for them. We want to justify them as thoughtful reactions to difficult dilemmas. That's pretty much what ethical decision making is all about and, when viewed in this way, regardless of what we call it, it becomes clear that we do some of this every waking hour of every day of our business lives. Some dilemmas are just a tad more difficult than others to navigate.

WHEN CASH RUNS OUT, BEHAVIORS CHANGE

In business, what to do when you're faced with a shortage of cash is a classic dilemma. It's conventional wisdom attributed to the U.S. Small

Business Administration (SBA) that 90 percent of all small business failures occur as a result of undercapitalization and cash flow problems. How that figure was arrived at is hard to fathom and it's likely nowhere near this level, according to economists at the SBA,[5] but anecdotally, seasoned business folks swear that cash flow problems often presage the death of a new business enterprise.

Jim Bildner, who in 1983 founded J. Bildner & Sons, a chain of upscale grocery stores, was experiencing tremendous success, if you measure success by growth rate. By 1986, he had opened more than 20 stores in Boston, New York City, Atlanta, and Chicago, hired more than 1,250 employees, and floated an initial public stock offering. But everything changed when, in 1988, he hit what he called "the wall." It "changed the world for us instantly and permanently," he writes. "Cash had run out. Our New York City operations were out of control (one sure sign was the time our employees there rolled a one-ton safe down two flights of stairs and through two glass doors so they could steal the money!), and our capital and lease commitments in those and other, remote markets were becoming unmanageable. Then, in mid-1988, we suffered catastrophic losses from those operations, which eroded our market value and—where it counts most—our customer loyalty, as inventory began to dwindle."[6]

For Bildner, running a fast-growth company had gone from exhilarating to "a desperate, intensely emotional, painful, and often public experience."

He's not alone. A lot of companies are thrust into awkward moments when they're forced to make decisions that result from a shortage of cash. When Planet Video, a chain of Midwestern video rental stores, wanted to expand the number of its stores aggressively, it needed $5 million for its ambitious growth plans. To attract investors' money, the founders figured they needed a top flight management team.

Victor Seyedin, president of the company, and his brother Nader, who headed up marketing, made the decision to hire expensive talent—including some former Blockbuster executives—to help it expand the business. "We really needed an organization to take it to a higher level," Victor Seyedin said.[7] With those top-notch employees came big salaries and the company's debt began to build. The founders may have justified their decision to fatten the payroll because doing so would in turn help them attract the money they needed for expansion. The video rental market experienced tough times in early 1997, however, and the brothers were unable to attract the outside financing they needed. When they filed for bankruptcy, Planet Video had about $12 million in debt. After selling the company's assets for roughly $10 million to Blockbuster, the brothers left the business. Victor, who along with his brother Nader lost their life's savings in the company, refers to it as "a sad story."

The Seyedin's story is not unusual. After all, "to make money, you have to spend it." All the more proof that shortage of cash makes you do things that you otherwise might not have. It forces you to make choices. When you're juggling the responsibilities of trying to run a business, those choices often cloud judgment. You find yourself coerced into making short-term fixes that you know will come back to haunt you, but you make them because the alternative at the time just seems too distasteful.

When Joe Burnieika joined with Robin Emerson and Larry Bearfield in 1994 to launch Burnieika Bearfield Emerson, an advertising agency, they grew the business successfully, at first. But a major client's defection created a dilemma: the agency either had to cut costs by laying employees off and risk not being able to complete jobs quickly in-house if business came in, or keep them on staff even if it meant a big hit to the bottom-line while they tried to attract more business. Payroll had increased from 40 percent to 55 percent of expenses. "We should have let people go and hired freelancers as we needed them," Burneika said in hindsight.[8] But he convinced himself that if he could only get one more good client locked in, he would have solved the immediate financial crisis. So, according to reports, the agency started underbidding on projects and found their margins eroding from a range that once hovered between 5 percent and 8 percent down to 4 percent or less. They weren't able to bill enough to make payroll. Plus, most of the less profitable clients were paying late—in closer to 90 days rather than the industry norm of 45. Debt piled up and the agency closed its doors in the fall of 1996.

Had the founders made the decision to cut staff at the first sign of trouble, they still might not have weathered the storm. But when you're faced with a decision about whether to lay people off or do everything within your power to try to make things work, you sometimes find yourself choosing to do things that you know in the long-term may not be good for the business. You start doing things you never could have imagined doing.

Who could have imagined that in March 1996, the Minnesota Department of Revenue would raid the Minnesota-based Sytje's Pannekoeken Huis Family Restaurants for unpaid sales tax equal to $300,000? The owner of the Dutch-motif pancake houses was facing all sorts of pressure since his ambitious growth plans hadn't panned out. Then, after the company lost $2 million in 1994, its franchisees stopped paying their franchise fees, alleging the owners' too-ambitious expansion plans led him to pay too little attention to their needs. After the raid, revenues dropped by 50 percent to 60 percent and within six months the company liquidated its remaining assets.[9]

The owner "was really intent on an acquisition strategy, but he didn't have his base covered," said a marketing consultant who worked with Pannekoeken in 1993 and 1994. The fact that the company had been losing money every year since 1991 couldn't have helped. The CEO may have seen expansion as the only way out of financial troubles, but then because he didn't have the cash to run his business effectively on a day-to-day basis, he apparently made decisions that proved fatal to the business.

Not every CEO of an undercapitalized company makes bad decisions. In fact, being strapped for cash forces CEOs and managers to be creative and careful. When Barry Keesan was in the process of expanding Logical Operations, a management training company in Rochester, New York, into the publishing business, he found himself woefully undercapitalized. "I needed close to $1 million but only borrowed $235,000, for which I pledged all the collateral I had, including my house," he said.[10] Consequently, Keesan says he and his managers were "forced to get even smarter in our core business, so we could generate more cash." They began offering equity in the business rather than huge salaries to new employees and found that equity was a more effective compensation tool anyway. Being undercapitalized, Keesan says, "did make us smart and efficient. We became the largest provider of training materials for the computer industry." The company was later acquired by Ziff-Davis.

When CEOs like Keesan face down undercapitalization problems, they have tough decisions to make. Undercapitalization in and of itself doesn't spell doom as long as cash flow is strong. Fortunately for Keesan, he was able to focus on revving up the cash flow in his core business to cover his undercapitalized expansion.

But when cash flow isn't there, a business owner can really find himself thrust into a corner and forced to make decisions he otherwise could never imagine making. "You live or die on cash flow," says Norm Brodsky, a columnist for *Inc.* magazine and the owner of a series of successful businesses. If, as a business owner, you don't make sure that you have cash coming in the door, says Brodsky, you're going to have to worry "about losing control of your situation, about decisions being taken away from you, about being forced to do extreme and unwise things just to stay alive."

"Going without pay is the least of it," he continues. "Many people stop paying their withholding taxes, which is not only illegal but stupid. Between interest and penalties, there is no more expensive money in the world. Meanwhile, your creditors are banging on your head because you can't pay your bills in an orderly fashion. It's a nightmare."[11]

WHEN CASH ISN'T COMING IN, DO ETHICS GO OUT THE DOOR?

But when you're facing a cash-flow crisis, does that mean your ethics have to go out the door? That's the question a CEO of a fast-growing company was facing when he found himself three weeks away from a payroll he knew he wasn't going to be able to meet. Just about this time, a check for $94,000 crossed his desk. He knew that amount was more than enough to cover the full payroll for his 50 employees, which meant his 6-year-old company would live to see another day, at least until the next payroll came around.[12]

The problem was that the check had accompanied an order from a customer who wanted a customized version of the software product his company made. The CEO knew that his organization would not be able to deliver the customized software product with its current staff and capabilities.

But he didn't want to miss payroll either.

Once, earlier in the company's history when paychecks were delivered late through no fault of his own, half of the employees had freelance jobs lined up by the end of the weekend. This event was fresh in the CEO's memory and he just knew that if the employees caught wind that he was going to miss making payroll, they would make a bee-line for the exit. The market for software programmers was strong and their services were in demand.

To make a decision, the CEO decided to lean on his top managers for advice—which, not surprisingly, varied widely. The chief financial officer, responsible for keeping tabs on the company's dwindling cash flow, wanted to cash the check right away. The head of sales shared that view, but then his compensation was tied to revenues. But the head of customer service thought it was a terrible idea to take and cash the check. It was, he thought, a sure way to anger a big customer if they took money for something they couldn't deliver.

It's no shock that the managers' advice came from what was in their own best interest. But what never came up in the discussion was whether misleading the customer was the ethical thing to do. Was it right?

Still, the CEO—with check in hand and a payroll coming due— had to make a decision. And he was no clearer on which way to go: Take the job and test the stress points of an already stressed workforce? Or turn it down when it was the only sure money on the table?

"This guy's having to listen to everyone and make up his own mind, which is the work of the CEO," says Sharon Parks, associate director of the Whidbey Institute on Whidbey Island in Washington, who was also part of the team who devised the ethics curriculum at Harvard Business School. In *Common Fire: Leading Lives of Commitment in a Complex World* (Beacon, 1996), Parks and her coauthors stress the importance of inner dialogue. "You'd be amazed at the number of people who have no insides. They're just always reacting, responding out there and they don't listen inside. And without that you don't get conscience, you don't get the reflected life, you don't get the moral life, you don't get the ethical life, because these require interior reflection which is not just a conference with one's self or with one's God, but with all the voices that come into play in a kind of inner board meeting. Conscience is made up of a dialogue of many voices."

In spite of the time crunch he was operating under, the CEO *was* trying to listen to his conscience. In a concrete way, as he was trying to make a decision he was trying to hear all sides and do what Parks refers to as the work of a CEO. He recognized that *part* of the world of business is that there are real people who depend on you. But the CEO knew there was no one right answer. The tyranny of difficult ethical decisions is that they're isn't always a clear right and wrong.

For four days, the CEO agonized long and hard, wrestling with the implications of each decision and the impact it would have on his company and his employees. He considered the advice of his senior managers. He replayed every imaginable voice advising him to take or turn down the order.

His solution? He took the check for $94,000, but he didn't cash it. Instead, he placed it inside a folder and filed it away. "When you're dealing with a large corporation like this," he reasoned, "at the top level they're really only talking concepts. It's not until you get into the field and deal with their people and what their expectations are that you really understand what they expect."

The CEO had decided to lie. Maybe he'd convinced himself that because he hadn't cashed the check, it wasn't really a lie. After all, he knew it would take some time to spec out the project, so he was really just buying himself time to see if he could find another way to get money in the door to cover the payroll that he would have to meet in 23 days.

"I figured if I could string these guys along for just three or four weeks while I'm figuring out what they really want, that would at least give us a chance to cover ourselves," he says. The CEO never stopped to think about whether it was right or wrong to deliberately mislead this prospective customer. In the midst of a cash-flow crunch, he thought he had made a sound management decision.

His reasoning is not an unusual one in business. Some company owners argue that there's no such thing as ethics in cash flow. It's business pure and simple. "The whole concept that there are ethics involved in cash-flow decisions is ludicrous," says the president of a small company in northern California.[13] "It is a fact of life that with a small, fast-growing business without lines of credit or large capital backing, you have to make choices. The only ethics involved are that you don't try to snake out on anyone or hide from them. It is also a fact of business that every time we extend credit to someone, we are taking a risk that we won't get paid or will get paid late."

But others in business find such an outlook disheartening. "I really hate to hear anyone say there are no ethics involved in the question of paying on time," another California company owner says. "To me, it boils down to, Does your word mean anything? I've run up against clients who had [that kind of] attitude . . . and I was careful not to extend credit to them again."

Even when you consciously decide not to renege on someone "or hide from them" you are in effect making an ethical decision. You've decided that in the course of doing business, there are some things that are just not right, or better, that you just won't do. You understand how business works, certainly. But within the context of that understanding, you've made some thoughtful decisions about how to run your affairs. The risk is that others might not act within the same code of behavior, but in your day-to-day business dealings, you still try to act in a way that minimizes that risk.

By the same token, if, for some reason you decide to suspend your own rules of behavior upon occasion, that too is an ethical decision; you've weighed the options, assessed your situation, and made a decision. The CEO with the $94,000 check needed to decide, given what information he had, how he was going to act.

Edwin Hartman, a professor in the faculty of management and the department of philosophy at Rutgers University, observes that "business ethics require an understanding of business, as one cannot make ethical judgments about an act without this sort of understanding of its context, and in particular its purpose."[14] It's an important observation. For ethics to seem anything other than abstract or judgmental, they must be grounded in a clear understanding of how your business works. Otherwise, it's easy to dismiss ethics as having no bearing on how you run your business affairs at all.

What happened to the CEO who took the check for the custom software project? For the next three weeks, he and his top managers engaged in every tried-and-true business practice they could to help their cash flow. They went after every receivable and slowed down every payable. The CEO contacted every large customer, telling them that even if the amount they owed seemed small, paying it would have a substantial impact on the CEO's company. "I expressed a sense of urgency without letting on how dire the situation really was," he says.

Simultaneously, the CEO and his managers started meeting with the customized-software product customer to spec out the project and learn exactly what they'd be facing should the $94,000 project really come to be. But it never did.

At the end of the second week, all of the company's efforts to bring in cash were working. They had raised sufficient money to cover the payroll, now only a week away.

"Exactly at the point where I knew we had managed through our cash-flow crisis and where we really knew what we were getting into," the CEO says, "I went to the customer and returned the check, telling them that I couldn't fulfill that commitment." The CEO's decision to bluff the customer while he tried to improve the company's cash flow had worked.

"Our client was surprised when we returned the check," says the CEO, "not because we didn't cash it but because they thought we'd keep the money and try to snake out of repaying it somehow. In the type of business we're in, there's a lot of maneuvering that goes on."

Were the CEO's actions really that big a deal? When you run a business, you make compromises every day. Sure, this CEO took the check for a job he knew he couldn't deliver, but he reasoned that if he didn't cash it, he wasn't really taking the prospective customer's money. What's more, his decision turned out to have had no ill effects on his company or its employees. He bluffed. All right, he wasn't exactly truthful in how he represented his company's intentions to the prospective customer. But this is a business he's operating, not a Sunday school class. Besides, don't forget, in this CEO's type of business, "there's a lot of maneuvering that goes on." *C'est la guerre.*

What the CEO failed to do was to put himself into the position of the prospective customer. That's the big issue here. How would he have felt if he had been strung out for several weeks believing that his $94,000 check was a good faith investment in goods that would be delivered? It's a common enough failing. Most people in business have found themselves thinking ill of or bad-mouthing a customer that hasn't paid its bill in three months. And what about those vendors who've committed to do a job that, as it eventually becomes all-too-painfully clear they had no business taking on? Maybe they too needed the cash. And those horror stories about how long the government takes to pay its contractors? The ethical issue comes into focus when you remind yourself that you could be one of those companies being stiffed, misled, and strung out. Ah. Now, it becomes clear why it's appropriate to step back and ask yourself and your management team the tough ethical questions that go hand-in-hand with managing a less-than-virile cash flow.

Whether and how we address such questions can determine whether we will ultimately engage in bad business practices. And, in time, those bad business practices can become acceptable behavior in whatever type of business you're in. That's the danger of compromising your ethics when faced with what seems an insurmountable cash-flow challenge.

You find yourself "being forced to do extreme and unwise things just to stay alive."[15] This software CEO who had gotten the $94,000 check was lucky. He was able to bend the truth and in the end was able to get enough cash coming in the door to keep his business running. But while he's still in business, who knows what damage he's done to the culture within his company. Do his key managers now trust him? He lied to a customer; why not to them? And if the key managers can't fully trust the boss, isn't it only a matter of time before the rank and file employees follow suit? When you plan in the mud, you get muddy.

What's at stake in such decision making reaches far beyond the individual ethics of any one CEO. "To rationalize that I cannot do anything about the state of business, because I am just a [fill in your position here] is ignorant, cowardly, and incorrect," asserts Frank Navran, a senior consultant with the Ethics Resource Center, in Washington, DC. "The only way the state of business will become more ethical is through the commitment of individuals at all levels of organizations to the highest ethical standards: CEOs who refuse to play cash-flow games with other people's money, leaders who tell their key employees the truth, vendors who accurately communicate their capacities, and employees who understand that anything less than the ethical choice is unacceptable."[16]

Your Behavior Can Transform Your Workplace

It's easy to dismiss the observations of outside observers who aren't in the trenches every day trying to tough out what it takes to sometimes grow a business. Don't dismiss them. Instead, perform a simple test:

Ask yourself how you would feel as a businessperson on the receiving end of the action you're about to take. If you'd feel it was wrong or unethical, chances are it was. Sure, business is tough and it often takes a tough hand to steer a business toward a successful course. But you needn't compromise your ethics in the service of your toughness.

Jim Collins and Jerry Porras observed in *Built to Last: Successful Habits of Visionary Companies* that core values "are the organization's essential and enduring tenets, not to be compromised for financial gain or short-term expediency."[17] For this to work, the authors write, a company must "take steps to make the ideology pervasive throughout the organization." Only then can the core values of any company "represent more than just a bunch of nice-sounding platitudes—words with no bite, words meant merely to pacify, manipulate, or mislead."[18]

The company you build will ineluctably reflect the ethics that are implicit in your own behavior. The company's culture will always embrace the values you hold. If you're willing to sacrifice doing the right thing for expediency's sake, so will the organization you build. What you say and what you do must correspond, or your words will ring hollow.

Don't confuse this type of behavior with anything labeled "soft" in today's rough-and-tumble business world. Some of the most ethical businesses around are run by tough leaders. You don't even have to be particularly well-liked by your employees to gain their respect. It's not bad to be loved; it's just not as critical as being respected.

"While we prefer to respect and to love our boss, if we can choose only one of those, most of us would choose to respect the boss and not love him, rather than to love him and not respect him,"[19] the psychologist Abraham Maslow said after spending a summer observing a small technology company in California.

A sure way for a business owner or manager to gain that respect is to make sure that even when facing the thorniest of dilemmas, that owner's or manager's actions don't undermine the values upon which he's trying to build his company.

3

Just Because It's Legal, Is It Right?

I t's very possible for an owner or manager of a company to make a perfectly legal decision without ever exploring the ethical aspects of the decision. That's not to suggest that making a decision that is legal is inherently unethical. It's just that sometimes the law gives us an excuse to ignore whether the action we are taking is right or wrong.

The bankruptcy laws in the United States are a perfect example. In theory, they're a wonderful tool that give troubled business owners the opportunity to turn their businesses around rather than go under. When a company files for protection under chapter 11 of the bankruptcy code, it can keep its creditors at bay while it tries to work out a plan to reorganize itself so it can overcome its financial troubles. In theory, this is a good thing, because if the business emerges from chapter 11 protection rather than liquidating its assets in a chapter 7 bankruptcy filing, the chances are that creditors will ultimately be paid and the company itself will continue to contribute to the economy by creating jobs, paying taxes, and engaging in commerce.

There "are many reasons why a business gets sick, but they don't necessarily mean it should be destroyed," observes Judge James A. Goodman, the chief bankruptcy judge for the district of Maine. Hundreds of thousands of businesses that at one time or another had financial difficulties survive today as the result of chapter 11 proceedings. They continue to contribute to employment, tax revenues, and overall growth. It's counterproductive to destroy the business value of an asset by liquidating it and paying it out in a chapter 7 if that company shows signs of being able to recover in a reorganization. As for creditors, one of the provisions of the bankruptcy code is that in order for a reorganization to be confirmed, the creditor must get not less than he or she would have gotten in a chapter 7 liquidation. So why not go through with the reorganization?"[1]

Judge Goodman argues that in spite of the fact that 80 percent of businesses that file chapter 11 protection never make it out of bankruptcy, the fact that 20 percent do makes the bankruptcy laws all the more worthwhile.

"If a doctor had a 20 percent success rate with terminal cancer cases, you'd say, "That's incredible!" Well, that's what we've got— companies that are terminal. We take the nearly dead and show them how to operate better, and one-fifth survive. What's wrong with that?" the judge asks.

The fact that there are roughly 1.4 million bankruptcy filings a year hasn't helped calm the perception that bankruptcy is being used as a shield to keep those who owe from paying back those who are owed. But the reality is that, of those 1.4 million filings, the vast majority are personal filings rather than business filings.

According to the American Bankruptcy Institute, while the number of bankruptcies filed from October 1, 1997, to September 30, 1998 was up 5.1 percent over the previous year and hit a record number of

1,436,964, the vast majority of those—96.7 percent—were personal filings. Business bankruptcy filings actually decreased by 15.1 percent from the previous year to 47,125.[2]

Regardless of the numbers, the perception remains that the number of businesses hiding behind bankruptcy laws rather than repaying their debts is endemic. Those who are involved closely in such cases, like Judge Goodman, argue that this perception is not accurate.

"Of course there are abuses," says Judge Goodman, "but in my opinion having been on the bench as a judge for 17 years and having practiced bankruptcy law for 20 years before that, the percentage of abuses is minimal. It's almost nil."[3]

But when a company fails, does the owner of that business have an ethical responsibility beyond the laws to make good on all of his debts, even if it means paying back creditors after the business has ceased operations? After all, after a company owner liquidates the assets of his business under chapter 7 bankruptcy protection and uses whatever proceeds are raised to pay off debtors, he can turn around and start a new company without ever paying off the people or businesses he owed money to when the prior company went bust.

Or are the bankruptcy laws, which forgive the business owner from the responsibility of paying back all that is owed, enough punishment? While it's perfectly legal to go out and start a new business without regard for past debts owed, some owners have made the decision that that's not enough, that they have a responsibility to make good on their past debts. And sometimes, the whole question gets mucked up in what side of the owing fence you're on.

ARE LAWS ABSOLUTION FROM HAVING TO THINK?

Forget whether or not you should have the responsibility to pay back your debts for a moment. The whole area of bankruptcy protection raises a far more interesting issue. And that's that it's a prime example of how laws and regulations, however well-intentioned, have resulted in a nation of business owners who are forgiven from having to think through the implications of their actions. If the law allows such and such behavior, the argument goes, then that's what I'm obligated to do—no more, no less.

Well, fine. But somewhere along the line, were business owners absolved from having to do some hard thinking on what their actions might mean? What they might say to the business community? What they might say about us and how we want to be perceived? Remember, this business community is likely one in which, post-dead company, you're going to be operating for a long, long time.

Now, don't get me wrong. I'm not suggesting that the laws are wrong or that after thinking through the meaning of your actions you might not decide to do precisely the same thing as you would have done had you just blindly followed the letter of the law.

When did we become a nation of people like Ilsa in the movie *Casablanca,* who looks longingly into Rick's eyes and sighs, "you'll have to do the thinking for both of us." Please. Just because the law makes it so doesn't mean we shouldn't have to think long and hard about our actions, just as we'd do in any other aspect of our business.

Be real, I can hear you saying it. (Or thinking it silently to yourself as you roll your eyes.) Who wants to sit around and participate in self-flagellation sessions where you go over in painful detail everything you owe to everybody you've disappointed—your customers, your vendors, your employees, your creditors, and not least, yourself? Especially when you're in the midst of something as painful as losing your business and everything you built? I can think of few takers for the role. It's only when you're on the other side of the fence—when you're one of the ones being stiffed—that you spend time wondering loudly why the bankrupt business owner doesn't think about doing the right thing.

That's pretty much what happened to Daniel J. Driscoll, the owner of Darlyn Development Corp., a $4-million general contracting company in Marlboro, Massachusetts, when he found himself looking at the cover of the November 1995 issue of *Inc.* magazine. There, staring out from the cover with a plate of roasted chicken with all the fixings was George Naddaff, the entrepreneur who discovered Boston Chicken, at the time a fast-growing restaurant franchise success story that in 1993 had become one of the hottest public offerings on record.[4]

Mr. Driscoll was incensed. So he took pen to paper and wrote the magazine a letter. In part, he wrote: "While I find it wonderfully motivating that one business can flourish because of the ideas and actions of Mr. George Naddaff, I also find it infuriating that the same man could flaunt to the business world that he had $14 million to invest in a new venture, when he has not paid small businessmen like myself for his business ventures that failed." When asked about that failed venture in that November 1995 article, Naddaff told *Inc.* senior editor, Joshua Hyatt: "I'd like to forget about it."[5]

"Why should a man who has all the money he did be able to walk away from a million-dollar debt?" Driscoll asked. "They should make it illegal. If you have the funds to pay your debt, then you shouldn't be able to walk away. . . . When he realized that his concept wasn't going to be the next Boston Chicken, he pulled the plug on it and fucked everybody."[6]

Naddaff and his partners at Olde World Bakeries, the corporation which owned Coffee by George, had invested roughly $5 million in the drive-through coffee kiosk concept before they realized it wasn't going to work. They decided to liquidate the business and arrived at an agreement to pay their creditors roughly 30 cents of every dollar that was owed. Driscoll was one of the creditors who had agreed to the payout.

Driscoll may have agreed to the payout, but he was none too pleased that it ever came to having to make this choice. What bothered Driscoll had nothing to do with whether Naddaff followed the law. Driscoll doesn't doubt that he did. But in spite of the fact that what Naddaff did was legal, Driscoll thinks he shouldn't have gotten off as easily as he did. Since Naddaff had the resources from his personal wealth or his other business dealings to make good on his debts, Driscoll believes that he should have been made to pay back his creditors in whole.

Going Beyond What the Law Requires

Regardless of the fact that the laws about how much of your personal assets are protected when a company goes out of business vary from state to state, some business owners who have been in the same position as Naddaff say that they believe the right thing to do in such circumstances is to go beyond what's required by the law to make good on your debts.

In 1985, Hawkeye Pipe Services Inc., a manufacturer of pipes for oil rigs, went out of business. Its founder, Bill Bartmann, owed more than $1 million to creditors. But Bartmann says he decided not to reach a liquidation agreement as Naddaff had with creditors. Nor did he file for bankruptcy. Instead, he decided that he would pay back all the money he owed, no matter how long it took him to do so.

"I was born and raised in Iowa, and back in the Calvinistic Puritan Protestant work ethic kind of environment, you were supposed to pay your bills," says Bartmann, who went on to found Commercial Financial Services Inc. (CFS), which in 1998, was a roughly $1-billion debt-collection company based in Tulsa, Oklahoma. "It just seemed inherently wrong to try to escape by using a law—granted, it was a valid law, and I am a lawyer—as an escape hatch or excuse. It just didn't seem the proper thing to do."

After he closed the doors on Hawkeye Pipe Services, Bartmann says it took him two and a half years to pay everyone back in full. But he says he did.

"You know the American capitalistic system is the neatest on the globe," says Bartmann. "It's a wonderful environment to allow people to go out and assume the risks and rewards of life. Now, people understand the reward side very easily. I don't think they understand the reciprocal side is that they should be obligated to pay the piper if indeed there are any assets with which to do that. The question is do they have a responsibility beyond the legal requirements?"

In October 1998, an anonymous letter was written to CFS's bond ratings agencies which questioned CFS's collection rates. Bond ratings were pulled and CFS was cut off from that source of revenues. Bartmann resigned as CEO in late October 1998 and on December 11, the company filed for bankruptcy protection. Bartmann continued going into the office every day as a consultant for the company for the fee of $1 per year. But by late January, according to local press reports, he sent an e-mail to CFS employees saying that his daily presence at the company "had the potential of creating a conflict in how the company is run." In late June, it was reported that employees were notified by e-mail that the company was closing its doors. It remains to be seen if Bartmann has any intention to make sure that all of the debtors owed money by CFS are paid back in full should the company not reemerge from bankruptcy protection.[7]

Chris Graff is another company founder who thinks company owners have a responsibility that goes beyond what the law requires. Or, at least he believed he did. Graff, is the president of Marque Inc., a successful ambulance manufacturer based in Goshen, Ind. But in a previous business, Graff didn't have such good fortune.

His furniture-making business, Geste Corp., went out of business in 1989. Graff auctioned off the company's assets, but, he says "After the auction, I didn't have everybody paid off. I was about 10 grand short. So I went to work and paid it back out of my income." Graff says it took him roughly four months to pay back the money that was still owed.

"I guess it's just a moral or ethical issue for me," he says. "When we make a decision to do something, we should be able to explain that decision in the same way to anybody who asks, be it our spouse, our business partner, an employee, a creditor, or a customer. I have to sleep at night."

Beyond their take on whether it was moral or not, Bartmann and Graff were oblivious to the fact that their efforts to pay back their creditors all the money owed could have very practical aspects to it. "I understand how people view bankruptcy," said Bartmann. "I guess I rationalized it pretty quickly that although I was eligible to take the easy cure, to do so would forever taint me with that stigma."

As a result of going through the difficult chore of paying back all the money he owed his creditors, when Bartmann was trying to secure working capital for CFS, he used his earlier act as reassurance that "lending me money now again is the safest risk you're ever going to take."

How Business Works

The reality though is that paying back your creditors in full even when you don't legally have to isn't a guarantee that you're going to be able to get money from creditors or investors when you need it for a new venture. Nor does not paying creditors back anything beyond what you're required to by law mean you'll never secure financing again. Naddaff has been able to raise capital for several business ventures after Coffee by George ground to a halt after he'd operated it for one year.

Even though he's been successful beyond his Coffee by George experience, Naddaff still seems to understand Driscoll's anger. "If I were sitting where he was sitting, I'd feel the same way," says Naddaff. "We just decided after opening up two units that this was a concept that would not work out to fast growth. I tried to be fair to everybody and spread around whatever assets there were after selling everything off."

Those assets that he spread around belong to Olde World Bakeries which was a corporation Naddaff had set up which owned the Coffee by George business. Only those assets were relevant when the company went under and it came time to liquidate the assets and try to pay creditors off. "Why would I take money from a company that I own and pay the debts of another company that is owned by me and several different people?" Naddaff asks. "It would be like disrupting the entire business system in the United States."

Naddaff may find actions like Bartmann's and Graff's "honorable," but he hardly believes they're indicative of how business works in this country. "In America," he says, "if a business can't make it, the government allows an individual to end the life of the business. When these laws were put into effect, you have to assume, a lot of smart people gave thought to this."

Naddaff's take on his actions is that he did the noble thing by closing Coffee by George down as quickly as he could, liquidating its assets to pay off creditors as much as possible, and not running up any more debt or costing him or his partners any more investment capital.

DIFFERENT SIDES YIELDS DIFFERENT PERSPECTIVES

Driscoll, one of those creditors who settled for 30 cents on the dollar, just didn't think Naddaff did enough. But Driscoll doesn't take issue with the laws themselves that Naddaff could have used to protect himself. Nor does he seem to have a real problem with the fact that bankruptcy laws exist. Driscoll's problem, it seems, was that Naddaff hadn't suffered as much as he did when, back in 1989—six years before Coffee by George went bust—he'd filed for bankruptcy himself. As it turns out, Driscoll's earlier venture—Emerald Electric, a 50-employee, $7-million electrical contracting business—had failed. He filed for chapter 7 bankruptcy, then liquidated all of the company's assets. His problem with what Naddaff did stemmed from the fact that Naddaff didn't suffer as much as Driscoll thinks he did when he went out of business.

"When I went out of business, I lost everything—my house, the cars, the whole nine yards," says Driscoll. "I didn't shut my doors, walk away from a million dollars' worth of debt, and then go home to a $5-million house and a $100,000 automobile. When I went out of business everything went. I didn't have some 50-odd million dollars behind me and just decide, 'I'm not going to pay these people,' and close down another entity and walk away from it. If someone personally has the money, why should they be able to walk away and screw everybody? Where, when I did it, I didn't have any options. I didn't have choices—you know what I'm saying?"

A common argument among some seasoned business owners is that part of the responsibility for not getting burned by companies that go bust is to do enough due diligence on the companies you're doing business with, so you can gauge how much of a risk they really are. A pool-and-spa industry consultant in California, makes the point that while he feels sorry "for the company that gets nailed with a bankrupt customer, it is, in the final analysis, the responsibility of the supplier to weigh the loss potential against the possible gain in dealing with a corporation. All too often a company will jump at the chance to sell their products and services without due diligence."[8]

That might be an honest sentiment, but no matter how much due diligence you do, it's impossible to always determine when a business is likely to go bust owing you money. You do the best you can to trust that the people you're doing business with will stay in business and make good on their debts.

But what about the notion that everyone should suffer equally when a company goes under? The idea of writing a set of laws based on the premise that everyone should suffer equally when a company goes out of business just "doesn't make good common business sense," says Judge Goodman.[9]

That's a good point. For one thing, who's going to make the determination of just how much suffering is enough? And for another, one man's suffering is another man's . . . well, you get the point.

But tell this to a group of business owners and you're likely to get a visceral response on both sides of the argument. After reading the story of George Naddaff and Coffee by George, one CEO was incensed. The founder of a business that goes under should suffer at least as much as the folks owed money, this owner of a software development firm in Denver, argued. "George Naddaff is wrong and he knows it," he said. "The law may be on his side, but he's confusing what is legal with what is right. Just one question for you, George: When the lawyers arranged for your creditors to be paid 30 cents on the dollar, did you adjust your salary accordingly?"[10]

Still, Judge Goodman sees the fact that the U.S. Constitution holds that Congress should provide for a uniform bankruptcy act, where essentially debt is forgiven as a national policy, as a good thing. This "country was founded by debtors," he says. The authors of the Constitution "came from places where they were put in jail because they owed money. Our forefathers didn't want commoners like themselves thrown into debtors' prison if there was some other way out."[11]

You can find an equal number of CEOs who agree with this sentiment as those who don't. A CEO of an asset-management company in Dallas, sees the clear intelligence of a bankruptcy law that forgives failure. "You have to look at each bankruptcy individually," he said. "Too often we look at the past abuses of a few and often end up really hurting the ones that are truly using the system for what it was designed to do."[12]

But that doesn't address the fact that anger is a perfectly normal and common way to feel when it's you who are the one who's being stiffed. "We all want to feel bad for someone or a business that has had to file for bankruptcy," says the president of a Tampa-based debt-collection agency, "but how do you feel when you can't collect on an invoice and your accounts receivable are down the tubes?"[13]

Driscoll's experiences with companies going bust were unhappy ones, to say the least. First, when his own company, Emerald Electric, goes out of business, he takes a huge professional and personal financial hit. And then, when Coffee by George bites the dust, he's faced with not getting total payment for work he'd done for the business.

Given the ire he felt on both occasions, and the exasperating anger he felt toward George Naddaff for not paying him back in full, it's interesting that, unlike Bartmann and Graff, Driscoll didn't feel obligated to pay back Emerald Electric's creditors in full once he found success in Darlyn Development Corp., his new business.

Driscoll certainly had no legal obligation to take such action. But, like Bartmann and Graff, he could have chosen to.

SITUATIONAL ETHICS

If ever there was a prime example of *situational ethics* at work, here it is. In the less-then-perfect world of situational ethics, you can adapt what you hold to be ethical behavior based on how each event or circumstance affects you. Say, if you get burned in business and the laws do nothing to make you whole, well, then you can pronounce the person doing the burning as highly unethical or, at the very least, of questionable ethics. But if your business goes under and there's simply no cash left to pay back the folks to whom you owe money, why then you can hide behind the protection that the laws afford. Ah, sweet vindication. Using situational ethics allows you to miss the inconsistency between the way you behave, which you hold to be perfectly reasonable, and the way others are when they behave exactly the same way and you hold them to be wildly unethical.

One of the problems with situational ethics is that it gives people the ability to elevate and label unfortunate situations to the status of unethical ones. If he's been wronged, the wronged party may feel better if he can toss accusations of ethical misbehavior around. People in business find themselves in situations like this all the time. If you've got to fire a problem employee, that employee quickly becomes, at least to your mind, guilty of all sorts of unethical behavior. If your creditors are knocking on your doors for cash because you've been late paying or because they know your company's down on its luck and they'd better get their payments now, you start viewing these creditors as unethical vipers beating at the doors to pile on when you're down. And those customers who owe you money, but keep telling you they'll have a check in the mail as soon as their cash flow improves get elevated to the status of no good, unethical dead-beats. But the truth is that just because something feels unfair to you at some particular moment in time, doesn't mean that it's the result of an unscrupulous, unethical pattern of behavior. You just may not like it.

PERSONAL DECISIONS DEFINE BUSINESS BEHAVIOR

Much of how you behave in business comes down to personal deci-sions you make about what you believe is the right thing and the wrong thing to do. If you have to shut down a business, you might make the same choice that Naddaff and Driscoll did and liquidate its assets and then pay back creditors not a penny more than whatever agreed-upon percentage you arrive at. You could also follow suit with Bartmann and Graff and decide that you believe the right thing to do is to pay creditors back in full regardless of what the letter of the law requires. Driscoll is entitled to his strong opinions about what Naddaff did and how he should have behaved—even if Driscoll himself be-haved almost exactly the same way when faced with a similar situa-tion—but that doesn't by any means suggest that what Naddaff did when he shut down Coffee by George was unethical.

"This is a man who is upset, and rightfully so," says Naddaff. "Es-pecially if it hurt him in other ways. But it was a decision that was made by the board, who said, 'This business is not viable.' A brave man does it with a sword. The coward with a kiss. And that's the way it's done in business."

Indeed, when a company goes bust and there's no legal agreement to make full restitution to creditors, then it's up to the owner or founder how much he is going to go beyond the law. Does he think it's right to make good on debts? Like Bartmann and Graff, does he think there might even be an upside to future business dealings if he goes beyond the law and makes folks he owed money to whole?

Driscoll is hardly alone in feeling one way when he's owed money and another when he's the one doing the owing. We're all capable of taking a strong, yet diametrically opposed stand depending on what side of the issue we're on.

When Naddaff, for example, was asked what he looked for in entrepreneurs to invest in, he responded: "I look for the passion. I look for the commitment. I look for where this guy has been in his life. Is this a guy who has hocked his wife, his firstborn, his teeth, his contact lenses, his pacemaker, and his hearing aid? That, to me, is commitment. That's the guy I'm going to back. . . . I can see the sweat on his upper lip. Lots of entrepreneurs hock their houses. What's more sacred than a house? I like it when I hear someone has done that."[14]

George Naddaff may "live by the sword and die by the sword," but, like Driscoll, he's perfectly capable of seeing the same situation differently depending upon which side he's on. If he's looking to invest in someone, then he wants someone who's willing to put his personal assets on the line. But in the case of Coffee by George, when Naddaff's corporation was left owing creditors, that was a different case.

Here's the thing when it comes to situations like this. The easy thing to do is hide behind whichever side of the law or circumstances protects your interests the most. And that's fine. But the ethical thing to do is to acknowledge that that's precisely what you're doing, to give some thought to whether by your actions, you're behaving in a way that you believe to be right. It's perfectly reasonable to believe that business is a game, where sometimes you win sometimes you lose, but in all circumstances you're willing to play by the rules. You have to determine for yourself though, after careful thought, when you arrive at a point where rules be damned, whether you've got an obligation to set things right.

4

How to Make a Decision When You Don't Know Enough

O ne of the toughest things you have to do in business is make decisions based on incomplete information. Most intelligent people who want to make the best decision possible would try to collect as much information as possible before making that decision. But practically speaking, we all know that's often not possible.

Oh sure, if you waited long enough, you could really get a truer sense of the context and the complexity of any situation, but by then, it'd be too late. Your decision would be way overdue, the opportunity that stood before you would have passed, or the situation that needed addressing would just as likely have developed into full-blown crisis as much as it would have dissipated out of existence.

In a small way, we can see such indecision lead to minor inconveniences for a company. You need to hire a good manager, but there's some niggling little details about his background that make you not absolutely sure he'll be a good fit. So you wait and ponder. You hash the guy's credentials about. You talk to valued colleagues and mentors. You drag on the process as long as possible in hopes that somehow you'll someday have all the information you need to make the precisely right decision about this guy who, in the back of your mind, you keep thinking, might be just the person you need to reenergize your company and take it to the next level. A real rainmaker. A guy who can help take your business in directions that you can only partly imagine feasible. But there's that one thing that bugs you on his resume—an unexplained gap in jobs perhaps, or a history of moving around a lot more than you're really comfortable with. Still, you know, all things being equal, and given everyone you've seen, he just might be *the* guy, the big cahuna.

But you wait. And finally, when you've wrestled all your doubts to the ground and you trust your information and instincts enough to make the guy an offer, it's too late. He's gone. Your instincts that told you he might just be *the one?* Well, about a half-dozen other managers and CEOs thought so too, and scooped him up long ago.

Your indecision because you didn't have complete information cost you. The expressions "he who snoozes, loses" and "eat lunch or be lunch" are by now clichés of the cut-throat business world. But there's nothing cut-throat about having to make decisions based on incomplete information. It's something that every good businessperson has to learn how to do if he or she wants to stay competitive and to keep their business running.

Besides, it's the responsible thing to do. If you wait long enough, sure, many decisions will get resolved and you'll be absolved of having been the person responsible for taking that action that might not have turned out to be so good. But that's passing the buck, refusing to have the conviction to take action. And if you find yourself always in the position of hoping you won't be thrust into the position of having to make a tough decision, at some point, you're really going to have to sit yourself down and ask yourself why you got into this business in the first place. Put bluntly, making decisions based on less-than-complete information is part of most every job anywhere.

TAKING ACTION BASED ON YOUR CONVICTIONS

Many routine decisions you make will have ethical aspects to them that may or may not seem of huge consequence at the time. Even if it's something as simple as deciding how long to wait before paying an unpaid vendor's bill, you're making a decision that will have some effect on the person waiting to be paid as well as on his or her perception of what your actions say about you. But when you recognize that the decision you have to make is loaded with ethical implications—whether it has to do with something that will affect an employee's life, a customer's safety, a vendor's livelihood, or any myriad circumstances fraught with ethical nuance in running a business today—that's when the real tough choices begin.

None of this is to suggest that you should forego collecting as much information as possible to help make a decision. In "Ethics in Practice," an article he wrote for the *Harvard Business Review* in 1989, Kenneth R. Andrews observed that: "Responsible moral judgment cannot be transferred to decision makers ready-made. Developing it in business turns out to be partly an administrative process involving: recognition of a decision's ethical implications; discussion to expose different points of view; and testing the tentative decision's adequacy in balancing self-interest and consideration of others, its import for future policy, and its consonance with the company's traditional values."[1]

"But after all this," Andrews continues, "if a clear consensus has not emerged, then the executive in charge must decide, drawing on his or her intuition and conviction. This being so, the caliber of the decision maker is decisive—especially when an immediate decision must arise from instinct rather than from discussion."

Andrews' observation is instructive. A decision that has to be made based on incomplete information, or a lack of a clear consensus, says as much about the decision-maker as it does about the decision made.

This is why it's not surprising that decision making—taking action—is an act that can be seen as having a lot to do with the values of the person who is engaged in making the decision. Rushworth M. Kidder, the founder of the Institute for Global Ethics in Camden, Maine, writes in his book *How Good People Make Tough Choices: Resolving the Dilemmas of Ethical Living* that making decisions takes "moral courage—an attribute essential to leadership and one that, along with reason, distinguishes humanity most sharply from the animal world."[2]

To make ethical decisions, Andrews and others observe, you have to be able "to recognize ethical issues and to think through the consequences of alternative resolutions." You have to have the "self-confidence to seek out different points of view and then to decide what is right at a given time and place, in a particular set of relationships and circumstances." But most importantly, you have to have "what William James called tough-mindedness, which in management is the willingness to make decisions when all that needs to be known cannot be known and when the questions that press for answers have no established and incontrovertible solutions."

What businessperson doesn't like to think of himself or herself as having, whenever necessary, the "tough-mindedness" of which William James writes?[3] After all, when you've reached a level in business where you believe you truly are competent to do your job, don't you want to think of yourself and have others think of you as someone who's cut out to make the tough calls when the tough calls must be made?

Testing the Implications of Your Decisions

It's not like some thought hasn't gone into how tough ethical decisions can be made with less than complete information. There are any number of exercises that seasoned business-people can use to suss out what implications their actions might have. But often, when you're in the midst of the decision, it's difficult to see the implications unless you step back and think about the broader implications of your decisions.

Some of these solutions are simple and straightforward and you're likely to have heard variations on them before. Norman R. Augustine, the former CEO and chairman of Lockheed Martin, for example, uses these four questions to gauge whether what he's doing is ethically correct:

1. Is it legal?
2. If someone else did "this" to you, would you think it was fair?
3. Would you be content if this were to appear on the front page of your hometown newspaper?
4. Would you like your mother to see you do this?

"If you can answer yes to all four questions," says Augustine, "then whatever you are about to do is probably ethical."[4]

Augustine's rules are simple. But Peter Drucker's rule is even simpler. Drucker, the management writer and professor, argues that when it comes to ethics, "the rules are the same for everybody, and the test is a simple one." He calls it the "mirror test."

As the story goes, the most highly respected diplomatist of all the Great Powers in the early years of this century was the German Ambassador in London. He was clearly destined for higher things, at least to become his country's Foreign Minister, if not German Federal Chancellor. Yet, in 1906, he abruptly resigned. King Edward VII had then been on the British throne for five years, and the diplomatic corps was going to give him a big dinner. The German ambassador, being the dean of the diplomatic corps—he had been in London for close to fifteen years—was to be the chairman of that dinner. King Edward VII was a notorious womanizer and made it clear what kind of dinner he wanted—at the end, after the dessert had been served, a huge cake was going to appear, and out

of it would jump a dozen or more naked prostitutes as the lights
were dimmed. And the German ambassador resigned rather than
preside over this dinner. "I refuse to see a pimp in the mirror in the
morning, when I shave."[5]

Ethics, says Drucker, requires us to ask ourselves "what kind of
person do I want to see when I shave myself in the morning, or put
on my lipstick in the morning."

While such wisdom is sage, for some folks such simple, practical
approaches just might seem to fall short when you're staring down a
complex issue, one that you know doesn't have one simple answer.
For such wrestling matches, you might need to ask yourself some
tougher questions about the decisions you are about to make.

In a remarkably clearly written and nonjudgmental essay titled
"Ethics Without the Sermon," written for the November/December
1981 issue of the *Harvard Business Review,* Laura Nash, now the director of the Institute for Values-Centered Leadership at Harvard Divinity School and formerly a professor at Harvard Business School,
presented a more detailed, yet still very straightforward set of exercises
that can be used to take measure of what implications any actions
you're about to take might have. She suggests that by asking yourself
a set of 12 questions while in the process of making a decision, you
give yourself a pragmatic framework against which to test the ethical
content of business decisions.[6] Before reaching a decision, Nash suggests answering the following 12 questions:

1. Have you defined the problem accurately?
2. How would you define the problem if you stood on the other
   side of the fence?
3. How did the situation occur in the first place?
4. Who was involved in the situation in the first place?
5. What is your intention in making this decision?
6. How does this intention compare with likely results?

7. Whom could your decision or action injure?

8. Can you engage the affected parties in a discussion of the problem before you make your decision?

9. Are you confident that your decision will be as valid over a long period as it seems now?

10. Could you disclose without qualms your decision or action to your boss, your CEO, the board of directors, your family, or society as a whole?

11. What is the symbolic potential of your action if understood?

12. Under what conditions would you allow exceptions to your stand?

"Using the questionnaire format," Nash explains, "executives first define the problem and then attempt to examine it from an outsider's perspective. Next, the decision makers explore where their loyalties lie. They consider both their intentions in making the decision and whom the action might affect. The executives then proceed to the consequences of disclosing the action to superiors and other respected parties. A final analysis involves the symbolic potential of the decision."

MAKING COMPLEX DECISIONS QUICKLY

Not surprisingly, how you make an ethical decision—based on as much information as you can gather—is rarely specific to your industry or business. Drucker observes that ethics "do not vary much— what is ethical behavior in one kind of organization or situation is ethical behavior in another kind of organization or situation."[7] That's a sound observation, especially when there's a tendency to respond to questions from outsiders about the troubling aspects of an action you are about to take with comments like, "You just don't understand my industry," or "It's much too complex an issue to explain." To responses like this, the rule that if you can't explain it, you likely don't understand it, is a good one to take to heart.

The Johnson & Johnson Tylenol case is a clear example of how complex decisions based on incomplete information can be made quickly. Johnson & Johnson decided, in 1982, to recall those 31 million bottles of Tylenol from store shelves after eight people in the United States had died from cyanide-laced capsules. The move cost Johnson & Johnson $240 million and cut its profit on $5 billion in revenues that year by almost 50 percent. The tampering was not the company's fault, but nevertheless it decided to act before it had complete information on what had happened. The product containers were redesigned and new tamperproof packaging was introduced.[8]

"I am certain that no text marketing analysis could quantify or even identify the factors that informed their strategy," Laura Nash wrote in her book *Good Intentions Aside: A Manager's Guide to Resolving Ethical Problems,* after she interviewed the top three officers at Johnson & Johnson involved in the Tylenol case. "From an economic and public relations standpoint, one could have made a very reasonable argument for keeping the product on the shelves: The contamination was not the company's fault, and did not appear to have originated from a Johnson & Johnson facility; this was an isolated incident, the result of aberrant behavior; the benefits of the product to the majority of the public vastly outweighed the injuries that might occur if the product remained on the shelves."[9]

The officers at Johnson & Johnson had to make more than 200 decisions within the first 24 hours of learning of the Tylenol deaths, Nash recounts. As we cited in Chapter 1, Johnson & Johnson was successful in making these decisions because it had been able to use its long-established corporate credo as a guide to determining the right thing to do.[10] "As one manager told me," writes Nash, "Tylenol was the tangible proof of what top management had said at the Credo challenge meetings. You came away saying, 'My God! You're right. We really do believe this. It's for real. And we did what was right.' "[11] But still, 200 decisions within the first 24 hours is no easy feat. Especially when there was likely still so much unknown when each of those decisions needed to be made.

WOULD YOU LIE TO SAVE
YOUR COMPANY?

And what happens when you need to make a decision based on incomplete information that might save your company, but in the process makes you face having to make the decision about whether or not to be totally truthful? Let's take the example of a business owner who was thrust into the position of having to decide if he should tell his auditors about a company-threatening problem—thereby ensuring what he was certain would be the business' demise—or lie to them and wait the problem out.

"I'm at my board meeting," the CEO of a $20-million company that repairs aircraft engines, told me, "and I get this fax from the airline saying that eight aircraft my company had repaired engine parts for were on the ground. They were not going to let the jets fly because the turbines went kaput. And they were saying that our parts had caused the problem.

"Within a couple of hours," he went on, "I get another call saying that another aircraft is downed by another airline in another country for the same reason. Then an hour later, another call. And then another. In all, 11 planes were grounded because of what they were saying were our parts."[12] The CEO knew that the airlines were going to have to lease aircraft to cover those routes and that if his company was eventually found to be responsible for the grounding, his company was going to have to pay the $40-million those replacement aircraft would cost. This turn of events would certainly sound the death knell for his company.

"Oh, sure, I'd had incidents in the past," the CEO says, "but nothing to this extent." In fact, his reputation for quality after decades in the engine-repair manufacture business was nothing if not superb. The company worked with 15 different airlines. The Federal Aviation Administration (FAA) has approved the company as a supplier. And so too had all the major aircraft-engine manufacturers.

The FAA had already received notice of the problem by the time the CEO had been notified, and it had started an investigation of the office located where the groundings had occurred. "If they wanted to," the CEO says, "the FAA could have decided to close not only the factory where those specific parts were repaired but all of our factories to scrutinize us, check our procedures, check all our people. Of course, that's what you want when you fly. You want to make absolutely 100 percent certain that the engines are safe. But for us as a business, such a companywide inspection would have been the end."

The CEO's imagination ran wild with what would happen if news of the investigation got out to all of his lenders. "I had short-term loans with about eight banks for an amount of money equal to my equity in the business," he says. "They could have pulled those loans."

The FAA hadn't yet notified his company, however, that it was going to take such action. And while the local press reported extensively on the aircraft groundings, the company was never mentioned in any of the articles published. Because of this, the CEO decided that it was a reasonable course of action for him to do nothing until he had more details on the specifics of the grounds. It seemed like a good, doable strategy for the near-term, except for the fact that by sheer happenstance, the company was in the midst of its annual audit.

When a company goes through an annual audit, as part of the process the CEO and the chief financial officer assure the auditors that they have been notified about any outstanding circumstances that might prove to have a negative financial impact on the company. "The document was sitting on my desk waiting for my signature," says the CEO. "I was going to have to decide whether or not to sign it or to tell the auditors about the extent of our problem."

So the CEO of this company was facing incredibly high stakes. If he was forthcoming on the audit statement about the situation he was facing, he knew he was likely to create a ripple that would crash his company to the ground and leave it in pieces. But the information the CEO had was vastly incomplete. He convinced himself it was far too early to put his company's existence, and the jobs of its hundreds of employees, in jeopardy. So he sat facing an overwhelmingly frustrating situation. "In my industry, there's a very tight code of ethics about the use of drugs or alcohol by a manufacturer's employees," he says. "But there's nothing that tells you how you're supposed to deal with reporting information like this."

The audit papers sat there waiting for him to sign. But he could see no clear guidelines on what to do.

Having to make critical business decisions based on incomplete, fuzzy, or inadequate information is not that unusual for a CEO today. Yet, the fast-paced economy doesn't allow for much hesitation. In fact, the CEO who can act decisively in face of the lack of complete information is often held in higher regard than the one who can't. You've heard the stories dozens of times of the CEO who can think and act fast on his feet. When, for example, you don't have all the financing you need to go into new markets, do you take the risk anyway, even knowing that there's no safety net if your foray into those new markets doesn't pan out? Do you hire new workers before you're certain that the new market can support them? Do you lease more factory space, thus increasing your overhead, without knowing for sure if those new markets are as much of a shoe-in for success as you've claimed to those workers, your board, your investors, or your lenders? You get the picture.

The CEO of the aircraft-engine manufacturing company was facing a huge decision, but he wanted to do what he truly believed to be the right thing. For years, he'd been able to build his business successfully and make decisions by asking himself how he could keep his business growing and profitable while simultaneously avoiding excessive legal or financial exposure. But now, that way of doing things didn't seem to be a clean fit.

When the fax telling him about the groundings came to him, he'd been meeting with his board of directors. So he went to them and asked for advice. "My directors advised against doing anything that would raise more alarm that we were out of control about the issue than necessary," he says. He then spoke with his company's lawyers and hired lawyers and consultants who had vast experience in dealing with FAA investigations. He gathered all of the advice given him and used it to make a decision about how to deal with the audit statement that sat in front of him.

The CEO didn't make the decision in a vacuum, observed one businessperson who worked with an insurance company in Georgia, after becoming familiar with the case. "Companies have boards of directors, in addition to outside professionals, to direct them in times where critical issues are at stake," he said. "If you doubt their ability to give wise counsel, you need to make some changes."[13]

The CEO of the aircraft engine repair company says that "When it came time to sign the representation letter from the auditors asking if I had any unreported information that would affect the financial performance of the company, I withheld the information. I consulted my lawyers and wrote that we had a problem and that we were on top of that problem. I didn't get any more specific about it. And they didn't ask."

Kenneth Andrews argues that the "way the chief executive exercises moral judgment is universally acknowledged to be more influential than written policy. The CEO who orders the immediate recall of a product, at the cost of millions of dollars in sales because of a quality defect affecting a limited number of untraceable shipments, sends one kind of message. The executive who suppresses information about a producer's actual or potential ill effects or, knowingly or not, condones overcharging, sends another."[14]

Still, the CEO's statement was not all that unusual for someone who was undergoing a pending investigation, says Lynford Graham, director of audit policy at the New York City office of BDO Seidman LLP. (BDO Seidman was not the audit firm involved in the CEO's company's annual audit.) "Since the investigation had just been started and no responsibility had been assumed by the company, it's pretty unlikely that anything more needed to be disclosed at that point," says Graham. Graham points out that it's not atypical for these kinds of broad statements to be included in the business's financial statements, especially if the events were not likely to affect the finances for the year in which the company's books were being audited. He points out that this kind of language has become almost boilerplate to account for the many possible things that a company might experience that could cause negative outcomes that aren't accounted for anywhere else in its financial statements.

That it was standard industry practice to essentially say nothing about nothing might have been true, but the CEO still had to struggle with how to make a decision without all of the information he felt he needed to know to make a good decision. "I was frustrated that we weren't in control of the problem," he says. "It was in control of us. It was far beyond us, far beyond us. One of my biggest fears was that the groundings wouldn't stop with those 11 planes and that it would spread to all the airlines. After a while I knew this wasn't likely to happen, but it was a real fear, and it still ate away at me."

It may have eaten away at him, but that wasn't enough for him to decide to disclose everything he did know at the time and, in turn, risk his company's life. "If you have a business that's going to react to remote possibilities, then everybody's going to be nervous, and nobody's going to be able to do anything," says BDO Seidman's Graham.

Many businesspeople would find this wise counsel. When a service manager for a computer maintenance firm in California, learned of this CEO's dilemma, he stressed that it would have been "irresponsible and foolish" for the CEO to have taken a different course of action: "Why should the CEO of a company, whose goal it is to make that company survive and prosper, release speculative information voluntarily that would certainly destroy his company? The CEO took the necessary legal precautions."[15]

And Graham does make a good point. What the CEO did do resulted in keeping the company going. "I didn't inform everybody about everything," the CEO says. "Of course, the situation would have been different if an engine had exploded in air."

The CEO doesn't believe—or doesn't remember believing—that a mid-air explosion was a likely event. But it's not all that clear. When the groundings occurred, some newspaper accounts speculated that there was a chance, an awful chance, that fragments of engines might break off, hit the fuselage of the aircraft, and cause the plane to crash. You'd think that would be a critical factor that the CEO would take into account. But it was one he chose not to let enter his field of vision. He was concerned that his bankers and workers might find out. But in telling me the tale of the event, several years after it happened, he says he never entertained the possibility that people's lives could be at stake. He might have been fighting hard to ensure the security of his employees' jobs, but shouldn't he also have worked in what his responsibility was to the passengers who would be boarding other planes that might have been defective? He says that that was the FAA's concern.

Other CEOs working in heavily regulated industries can understand such a reaction. One Colorado CEO with vast experience dealing with the Food and Drug Administration, commented that "as a person who has designed and manufactured to the Food and Drug Administration's 510 specification, I can tell you it is a little different world than the local Pizza Hut franchise. The regulators take all your options away for public safety (for good reason). You are beholden to them and their procedure. If there was a real danger to public safety, you can bet the FAA would have grounded the fleet."[16]

DOES PUBLIC SAFETY EVER OUTWEIGH BUSINESS SURVIVAL?

Even still, this raises an important question. When you're trying to make a decision based on incomplete information, do you have a moral responsibility to weigh the risk factor to the end users of your product, especially in a situation like this one where, however remote, lives are at stake? Johnson & Johnson is still heralded for their decision to recall those 31 million bottles of Tylenol. Johnson & Johnson's immediate response to the problem saved the Tylenol brand and won the company rave reviews. But there are actions that a huge company like Johnson and Johnson, with $5 billion in revenues at the time and dozens of highly profitable product lines besides Tylenol, can take that a $20-million company like this aircraft-engine repair manufacturer would never survive. Plus, in Johnson & Johnson's case, eight people had died. Here, planes were grounded. Not a single person had been hurt as a result.

The CEO did weigh the effect his decision would have on some of the people involved, such as his bankers and employees, but he didn't take into account those people who might have the most at stake: The airline passengers on those aircraft running on engines his company had repaired. As a consumer who flies regularly, uses Tylenol (perhaps a tad too much), drives cars, and eats food, I have this striking notion that standard ethical behavior cries for businesses—and those running the businesses—to consider the exposure that consumers face from their decisions. Remember Laura Nash's seventh question to ask from her "Ethics Without the Sermon": "Whom could your decision or action injure?"

One question is whether or not the CEO would have told his auditors anything different had he allowed for the possibility that airline passengers might be at risk, however remote. Probably not. And, as it happens, that might have been an acceptable course of action since the FAA deemed that his company was not directly responsible for the grounds. In fact, the FAA ultimately concluded that airline passengers were never at risk as a result of the problem. Still, airline passenger safety was not among the things he says he considered before deciding to sign the auditor's statement. It should have been.

"I can't imagine that a person directing a company in this business wouldn't be thinking about the impact on lives as the critical issue," reflected the Georgian insurance man.[17]

Granted, people who run fast-growth companies of any size can easily become so absorbed in the day-to-day activities that are involved in keeping pace that they can find themselves becoming desensitized to some of the outcomes their actions create. That doesn't, however, make it acceptable to become insensitive to circumstances where the consequences of their actions can be huge.

Making ethical decisions, observes Kenneth Andrews, "is easy when the facts are clear and the choices black and white. But it is a different story when the situation is clouded by ambiguity, incomplete information, multiple points of view, and conflicting responsibilities. In such situations—which managers experience all the time—ethical decisions depend on both the decision-making process itself and on the experience, intelligence, and integrity of the decision maker."[18]

When you're an experienced CEO who's spent his entire business life doing what he's needed to do to keep his company alive, growing, and profitable, it becomes too simple to take cover behind boilerplate language, standard operating procedures, or a regulator's responsibility. You easily forget that there are times when you must take into account far larger issues in your decision-making process.

The CEO of this aircraft-engine repair manufacturer defends the way he reasoned his decision. "What do I know about engines?" he asks. "As a businessman, I was looking at this in terms of my survival."

There's no question that making difficult decisions with incomplete or at best ambiguous information is difficult. But these decisions are made all the time, and they're made quickly. When faced with such a daunting task, a business owner or manager must lean on his experience, intelligence, and integrity to weigh as many of the implications of the choices he might make as possible.

While many decisions, such as the one facing the CEO of the airline repair manufacturer, seem on the surface to be primarily a decision about the financial health and survival of the company, the decision touches on more than the sphere of money. As the CEO saw it, remember, his largest concern was that if he had disclosed the aircraft groundings on the audit statement before he signed it, he was convinced he'd trigger a series of events that would cause his bankers to call their loans which would spell death for his company. But the CEO's decision also had implications for the people involved (the employees, the airline passengers), and, in this case, even the common good, since the safety of the flying public may have been at issue and seems certainly to be one important aspect that should have been addressed in the decision-making process.

It is often the case that these three spheres in which we find ourselves making ethical decisions—money, people, and the common good—in business overlap. The difficult task is finding a solution somewhere in the area of overlap so that the needs of each are weighed.

There are often no clearly right answers where every constituency's needs and concerns are met. But, even if they're ultimately dismissed, it becomes critical nonetheless to weigh these concerns in trying to make the right choice, especially if you want to remain the type of businessperson you want to be.

PART TWO

PEOPLE

We preach and talk a lot about caring for the people here. If you tell people you're going to care about them and you're going to support them, then when you get into a sticky situation, running away from it is the worst way to deal with it. Embracing it is pretty messy as well, but somebody's hurt, and you've got to do something.

—Owner of $14-million computer
consulting company

lready, after reading the chapters in the first part of *The Good, the Bad, and Your Business,* you can begin to see how the three spheres—money, people, and the common good—that come into play when making ethical decisions in business overlap. The goal, remember, is to try to address the needs of all three spheres as best as you can when making decisions. Just taking into account that your decisions can have an effect in all three areas is a start.

But as you'll see from the chapters in the second part of the book, issues dealing specifically with people in the workplace seldom have clear-cut answers. Your instincts—as a businessperson or empathetic individual—don't always drive you to make choices that in the long-run may be best for the people with whom you work. Still, those instincts may typically be more trustworthy than working from a checklist that treats people more like another cog in the business wheel than the productive workers they're capable of becoming.

But with the pressures brought on by a wildly litigious business world, you find that you're often not only going against your instincts, but you're also making decisions that may be neither in the best interests of the people involved nor best for the company's efficiency. Instead, it seems, more and more decisions get made out of fear of having a lawsuit slapped on you and your business. The laws and regulations certainly are meant to protect—and sometimes they actually do—but the biggest casualty of an increasingly litigious world is that often when the right decisions do get made, the person making those decisions hasn't thought through why they're the right ones. Instead, the manager, employee, owner, or other player in the business makes choices based on minimizing legal exposure. Sadly, that results in an atmosphere where people are pitted against one another from the outset in what can become a climate of fear and loathing in the workplace.

What adds to the complexity of making choices is that the boundaries between our personal and work lives have grown increasingly blurred. As a result, when you make a decision that involves what would formerly have been a very personal matter, you find that you're making that decision in what has become your main community—the workplace. So the challenge is to be clear when personal decisions might have an effect on workplace relationships. Such clarity may not change the choices you've made, but to understand more fully the impact of your decisions, it's important to think the implications through and to talk about them with the parties involved.

The chapters in Part Two are meant to help you think about how to connect with the people in the workplace and to recognize the obstacles that keep you from doing this. It's only then that you can begin to see the possibilities that people bring to the workplace rather than seeing them as objects in the way as you try to get your job done.

5

It's Enough to Drive You to Drink

O wners and managers of businesses are faced consistently with making decisions about when and how to help employees in the workplace. Sometimes, when these decisions are work-related, the decisions are relatively uncomplicated, ranging from deciding whether to accommodate an employee's need for more training to choosing whether to give some extra guidance to an employee who is on track for a promotion.

But often as not today, the decisions a manager or owner must make about helping an employee touch upon his or her personal life. It might involve allowing an employee to begin work at a later hour to accommodate the needs of a young family at home. Or it could involve any range of decisions a manager makes about whether and how to help an employee manage a complex series of personal needs.

And while the decisions about helping an employee with his or her personal problems are more difficult to address, managers will often give thought to trying to make accommodations. The workplace of today is rarely seen as a draconian place where workers are merely tools used in the production of profits.

"The fact that an employee is an employee does not lessen the duty of respect that he or she is owed," observes Yale Law Professor Stephen L. Carter. "To be polite only to one's superiors or equals in the corporate hierarchy is to violate several of the rules of civility that we have reviewed. One's employees are entitled to precisely the same degree of respect because . . . they hold a precisely equal share of God's creation."[1]

Not to put too practical an edge on Professor Carter's observation that employees are entitled to civil behavior, but perhaps the civility afforded employees has come partly from a recognition that workers who feel more satisfied are ultimately more likely to be more productive.

Intuitively, this might make sense to most of us, but there's also some empirical data to validate this notion. In a 1996 survey of Americans' attitudes about work at all sizes of companies, The Gallup Organization and *Inc.* magazine found that the "most critical factors bearing on employees' satisfaction and job performance seem to be the following:

- At work, employees have the opportunity every day to do what they do best.
- A supervisor or someone at work seems to care about them as people.
- At work, employees' opinions seem to count.
- Over the past year, employees had opportunities to learn and grow.
- The mission of their employer makes employees feel that their jobs are important.

- Employees have the materials and equipment to do their work right.
- Employees' companies are "family friendly."[2]

It seems that workers who feel like they're treated more like human beings in a business will not only be more satisfied at work, they'll also perform better. Go figure. This is hardly an earth-shattering outcome.

Still, to work well, employees must sense that the manager is doing more than just paying lip service to the latest trend in management style, that he's not just juicing up the latest buzz words ("employee empowerment!" "paradigm shift!") to win over a less-than-motivated workforce.

In *Good Intentions Aside: A Manager's Guide to Resolving Ethical Problems,* Laura L. Nash recognizes this when she writes: "Many of today's admonitions for business success, from closeness to the customer to empowering employees, rest on an other-enhancing point of view. If you understand the admonitions only in mechanistic terms, they will never be achieved. As one manager put it, 'I can establish an open door policy until the cows come home, but if I don't respect my employees, no one will willingly walk through that door.' "[3]

For employees to buy into the fact that a manager and by extension the business really cares about him or her as a person there must be some consistent actions that reinforce this view. Interestingly, when a company can achieve this perception among its employees, it's likely to be a more ethical workplace as well.

Kenneth E. Goodpaster, a professor at Harvard Business School, observed that "modern managers take the first step toward viewing the corporation as a moral environment when they cease to regard employees as mere tools for achieving corporate goals and begin to view them from a social perspective. The next step involves recognizing the value and dignity of each employee. By taking this step, the corporation assumes a moral viewpoint, which entails certain duties and obligations."[4]

The kinds of moral obligations that the corporation has, according to Goodpaster, include:

- Avoiding direct harm to employees.
- Respecting employee rights.
- Communicating honestly.
- Keeping promises and labor contracts.
- Obeying laws and complying with government regulations.
- Helping employees in need.
- Treating employees fairly.

But when you start considering the corporation as a moral environment, Goodpaster argues, these guidelines "must be guided by a larger vision of the community's well-being—one that accounts for both the welfare of the community as a whole and the welfare of the people in it."[5]

Don't get me wrong. I don't mean to suggest that helping employees, communicating honestly, or treating them fairly is a phenomena that is uniquely new to the workplace. Hardly. Good managers have known for years that such behavior will yield a more productive workforce. The reason that creating a moral environment for employees makes good business sense is that those employees will likely be more productive since the culture of the company mirrors their own beliefs about how they want to be treated and how they want to treat others.

There's nothing inherently "soft" about treating employees humanely. To give you an example of how strong business leadership skills can coalesce with humane treatment of employees, consider this story told by ethicist Paul F. Camenisch about his father's work running the Swiss Sanitary Milk Company:

> Dad clearly valued fairness toward his employees over an artificial camaraderie. But he could also be firm, even hard when he thought

it was appropriate. One day I stumbled into a heated exchange with a clearly agitated employee. Dad's explanation later was brief and to the point: "He lied to me. I fired him." And when Dad caught his man Friday filling up his own car at the company pump, Dad figured what such filching had probably cost him over several months and presented the man with the choice of paying up through payroll deductions or moving on. That may now sound unacceptably unilateral, even Draconian. But Dad was also very concerned, although helpless to provide any remedy, when the same man lost his small, hard-won house in divorce proceedings.

Dad's fairness was sometimes costly. In the days before insurance cushioned against all the ills of this life, one of his drivers' legs was crushed when his skidding truck met an oncoming Greyhound bus. Dad made room for him in the office until his legs healed, even though Swiss hardly needed another pencil-pusher. When the ten-gallon batch freezer had to be replaced with a much faster and more demanding continuous freezer, there was some question as to whether Frank—the freezer man for as long as I could remember—would be able to keep up with the faster equipment. But there was no question about whether Frank would still have a job.[6]

As a CEO or manager, while you may be demanding and tough-minded, it's more than likely that you instinctively want to help workers whose personal problems are interfering with their job performances.

It's easy to argue that such acts of altruism in the workplace are hardly unselfish. But as Rabindra N. Kanungo and Manuel Mendonca, observe in *Ethical Dimensions of Leadership*, "we need to recognize a common assumption held by psychologists that all behavior, whether directed toward benefiting one's own self or another, is energized by some needs or inner drives without which human behavior would simply not occur. It is, therefore, to be expected that altruistic behaviors must necessarily stem from an inner need state. These behaviors are directed primarily to fulfill the individual's objective or intention of benefiting others. In the process of meeting this objective, the behaviors do satisfy some needs of the individual, but the existence in human beings of the deeper-level need for altruism that is the source of these behaviors cannot be denied."[7]

In others words, while as an owner or manager, you clearly benefit on a personal level if you have a positive outcome to that natural desire to help employees whose problems are affecting performance, it doesn't diminish the fact that you're still likely to be trying to do the right thing, a good thing. Bottom-line? Just because you benefit does not take away the goodness of the act.

To Help or Not to Help

Still, while you want to help, how do you really know you can? After all, you're trained to run a business, that's your calling and it's also the context in which you know the employee. Doctors, psychotherapists, marriage counselors, and other professionals might be equipped to address the personal problems of your employees, but how do you know you are?

The drive to want to help, however, clearly outweighs the reality of the fact that you may not know exactly what it is that will help the employee with his or her problem. The result can be waking up to a harsh reality that sometimes trying to do what you perceive to be the right thing can take unpredictable turns.

A prime example of this involves the case of the $14-million computer consulting company whose owner had to make a decision about how far to go to help a troubled employee.[8] "Once in a while, people who are on the road go out and have a few too many, and that's fine," the owner of the consulting firm told me, recalling an incident involving one of his employees that happened a couple of years ago. "But one Monday morning, this particular employee just didn't show up for a project, and it was like, 'Oh no, where is he?' "

At the time, the company—which helps businesses design, install, and implement complex back-office software systems—employed 35 people and had $6 million in revenues. Only about a third of the business's employees work out of company headquarters. The rest of them, including this consultant who wasn't anywhere to be found, work out of their homes, since the job requires them to travel to the customer's site where they do their consulting.

The customer was anticipating that his new computer system was going to go live for the first time on this particular Monday morning. While a handful of people had worked on this consulting job, the consultant in question was the only one who was working directly onsite to make sure that the system worked. But then, he disappeared. "They were bullshit," says the CEO about the client's anger over the missed appointment. "Not showing up is pretty bad, but his not calling just made it worse."

After calling the consultant's sister to help track him down, the CEO finally found him by Wednesday morning. "Apparently, there'd been a lost weekend," says the CEO, suggesting that the consultant had been too drunk to get on the plane Monday morning. "It was a quart of gin, I guess."

The company "limped through the rest of the project," finishing up the best it could. When the work was done, the CEO made the decision that his company would eat half of the consultant's $200,000 fee.

That still left the CEO with a decision about what he was going to do about the consultant who hadn't shown up to do the job. When the CEO and his vice president of operations first made contact with the consultant, the man blamed the mishap on bad travel miscues, saying he'd overslept and missed his early-morning flight. By Saturday, he'd broken down and called the vice president at home to admit that he was an alcoholic. He was "basically crying and saying he needed help," the VP recalls.

Now that the CEO knew what he was up against, he faced the sort of agonizing decision that every employer dreads. Hire enough people and you're likely to grow comfortable passing certain judgments—right or wrong—on them: that they have particular skills or lack them, that they can rise to a certain potential or can't, that they fit in or don't. But the stakes are never higher than when what's under scrutiny is someone's personal behavior. Most CEOs, confronting what can often feel like life-or-death consequences, would rather sidestep such uncertain terrain altogether.

But every manager will, at some point, have to face the problem of a valued employee whose performance is impaired by a personal problem, whether it's substance abuse, an addiction to gambling, or a debilitating emotional problem. It can be a grueling decision for a manager to make. It's no easy task, even when you think you're doing the right thing.

Laura L. Nash tells of the experience Fred Roach, the CEO of Centennial Homes, had with such a case. Roach, she writes, "recounted the time that he had a cheating employee who was claiming sales he had not made. There was no doubt that the man had lied about his performance and had accepted commissions he hadn't earned. After speaking with the man, Roach offered him a choice between being fired or paying the money back and taking a three-month sabbatical without pay. If he would take the time 'to get his life together,' Roach promised to take him back. The employee went to counseling, took a rest, and came back as the top performer at the company, a record he still held three years later. Roach mused: 'Maybe I'm too easy, but I though he deserved a second chance. Work was part of his problem, so I forced him to stop working for a while. After all, I had once benefited from his overworking; I was partly responsible.' "[9]

When the Answers Aren't Clear

Remember the discussion of the mirror test and other factors suggested in Chapter 4 to do a quick test of whether your actions are ethical or not? Well, often, it's not quite that simple. Responsible "people sometimes lie awake at night *precisely because they have done the right thing*," suggests Joseph L. Badaracco, Jr., a professor of business ethics at Harvard Business School. "They understand that their decisions have real consequences, that success is not guaranteed, and that they will be held accountable for their decisions. They also understand that acting honorably and decently can, in some circumstances, complicate or damage a person's career. In short, if people like Hitler sometimes sleep well and people like Mother Teresa sometimes sleep badly, we can place little faith in simple sleep-test ethics."[10]

The CEO of the computer consulting firm felt he was facing just such a difficult decision. It's hardly rare for a manager to grapple with an employee who abuses alcohol. Roughly one out of every 12 full-time workers between the ages of 18 and 49 abuses alcohol, according to a report by the U.S. Substance Abuse and Mental Health Services Administration. When, if ever, does a manager need to step in? And what factors should be weighed in figuring out what to do?

The common assumption among many business owners and managers is that it's difficult, if not impossible, to fire an employee who has a medical condition such as alcoholism, even if he or she frequently misses work. The reality is that "absenteeism may be a basis for termination," says Jeffrey Klein, an employment-law specialist at Weil, Gotshal & Manges, a New York City law firm. "The fact of being a drinker and having a hangover and not being able to come to work is not protected. What's protected is alcoholism as a disability."

As far as the CEO of the computer consulting company was concerned, firing the alcoholic employee was never an option. "He made about as bad a mistake as you could make, but it was a first mistake," the CEO explains. "And people make mistakes of judgment all the time, even when they're not drinking."

The company, which was five years old at the time, had never confronted such a situation. But the CEO had had a previous close encounter with alcoholism. It so happens that his father is a recovering alcoholic who has been sober for 30 years. He talked to his father about the situation and his father's advice was to cut the employee loose. "His logic was that people have to hit rock-bottom before they can pull themselves up," says the CEO. "And what might seem like rock-bottom to me, which is how I thought the consultant was at the time, is really not rock-bottom."

That need for the individual to hit rock-bottom and take responsibility for his own actions is not unique to alcoholism. "Every therapist knows that the crucial first step in therapy is the patient's assumption of responsibility for his or her life predicament," psychiatrist Irvin D. Yalom writes in *Love's Executioner and Other Tales of Psychotherapy.* "As long as one believes that one's problems are caused by some force or agency outside oneself, there is no leverage in therapy. If, after all, the problem lies out there, then why should one change oneself? It is the outside world (friends, job, spouse) that must be changed—or exchanged."[11]

The CEO thought over his father's recommendation, but, he says, "I just didn't think I could do it."

The vice president of operations, who also was in charge of personnel issues, shared the sentiment. "I'll tell you honestly what went through my head," she says. "It was, What if this guy hits rock-bottom and kills himself, and it's my fault? I just couldn't take that kind of risk."

What's more, to abandon the employee felt like it flew in the face of the company's team-oriented culture. "We preach and talk a lot about caring for the people here. If you tell people you're going to care about them and you're going to support them, then when you get into a sticky situation, running away from it is the worst way to deal with it," the CEO says. "Embracing it is pretty messy as well, but somebody's hurt, and you've got to do something." Okay, you want to do something. But how do you decide what?

The CEO talked the situation over with the vice president of operations as well as his chief financial officer and vice president in charge of recruitment. Then he called the consultant and told him that he should find a treatment program, get help, and then come back to his job, which they would hold for him. The consultant listened and then enrolled in a two-week outpatient program near where he lived.

The company paid for the program out of pocket, since it had neither a short-term disability policy nor an employee-assistance plan at the time. The company also continued to pay the consultant's salary while he was away.

The consultant completed the program in short order and got back to work. And for about eight months, everything went fine. "Then he just didn't show up for work again," recalls the CEO. This time he cost the company about $5,000.

Once again, after consulting with his operations vice president, the CEO decided not to fire the consultant. They say it was a much more difficult call. But the managers decided they hadn't been tough enough with the consultant the first time around. So this time they needed to make clear to him what the consequences would be if he failed to show up for a job again in the future. They told him he had to get into and complete a residential treatment program—which would now be covered by the short-term disability insurance that the company by then had in place. Or else he had to clean out his desk. If he disappeared again, they made clear to him, he'd be fired.

While the consultant was relieved, he wasn't surprised that his employer continued to support him. "They're familiar with the disease," he says. "They understand it. They understand the lies. And they understand how difficult it is to live with."

But at least the way some substance abuse experts see it, it's not entirely clear that the consultant's managers made the wisest decision. "To put him through a treatment program is a very good thing, but once," says Dr. James W. West, vice chairman and former medical director of the Betty Ford Center, an alcohol- and chemical-dependency treatment center in Rancho Mirage, California. "After that, it's enabling. It sends a message to the person: 'Well, just keep trying to the best of your ability, but if you fall, we're here, and we'll take care of it. In spite of what it does to the company, we'll stick with you. We'll put you back in treatment and hope this will be the last time, but if it isn't, we'll be there again.' It's bad for the company, and it's bad for the employee."

What complicates matters for managers trying to make tough decisions about how far to go to help employees, is that you can get a wide breadth of advice from experts on what to do and what not to do. Not everyone would agree with Dr. West that giving this guy a chance after the first incident was solely an act of kindness. The basis of Employee Assistance Programs (EAPs), which many larger companies have as part of their health coverage, is that companies should "rehabilitate rather than terminate."[12] Most EAPs argue that it's not just a humane decision, but a cost-effective one when you consider the cost of terminating an employee and training a new one to take his place. Most small, young growth companies, however, don't have EAPs available to help them through such ordeals. Certainly this one didn't. It didn't even have short-term disability insurance in place at the time of the first incident.

If they had had an EAP program or participated in one of the growing number of EAP consortiums designed to service smaller businesses, they might have had clearer guidelines in place about how to respond. "Most companies don't have any policies that they use as guidelines," says Jeffrey Zeizel, cofounder and CEO of the Center for Health Resources, an EAP provider based in Woburn, Massachusetts.[13] "It probably would not have been unreasonable to fire this guy, but it probably was worth taking a chance on getting him rehabilitated the first time. When you're dealing from an EAP standpoint, roughly 75 percent of the people you're going to treat will have successful outcomes."

WHEN IS ENOUGH ENOUGH?

"But the ethical dilemma here is when is enough enough," says Zeizel. "EAP officials always want to help, but it's the alcoholic's responsibility to participate in their recovery. If they choose not to do that there's not a lot you can do. With certain people, it has to get worse before it gets better."

The struggle for the CEO of this consulting company was to decide how to do what he thought was best for the employee without jeopardizing the health of his company or risk losing customers because of the employee's behavior. His instincts told him to stick by the employee and that's not an unusual tact for a manager, especially of a young growth company.

Other CEOs would applaud this one's instincts, but believe he might have lost sight of a more important responsibility. The president of another technology consulting firm after learning of the details of this CEO's story says that he believes a business owner should "try to show a human touch, but not a hug." He admits, however, that making that distinction requires straddling another fine line. "I think of the shareholders and I think of why the business exists before spending its time and money on employee disasters. Never take one of these 'helping' campaigns off the business playing field and start helping the employee with your personal time or resources. That is not help."[14]

Still another CEO who was more paternalistic than the one facing the crisis with the alcoholic employee, would have done exactly the same thing because his employees are, he exclaims, "my people, my tribe."

In *Believers in Business,* her book on evangelical Christians in business, Laura Nash recounts another story, that of a crisis of conscience a Chicago manager had over an underperforming employee:

> We had a woman who was not getting the job done. I told her to take time off, and her parents had told her the same thing.
>
> It turned out she had cancer, and it wiped us all out. We really would have liked to let her go. We couldn't afford her nonperformance, and we felt she needed full rest. But as a Christian in business, I just could not do this. It had to be an act of faith to keep her on. So we just carried on; she worked three days a week, so we didn't give her full compensation. Now she's in full remission. It wasn't a disaster. That often happens. You think things mean disaster, but then you just get it behind you and it's all right.[15]

Such behavior and instincts are not unique to this manager. Many managers are compelled to act based on a sense of what feels right to them, what makes them feel good as human beings in business. But by the managers in the computer consulting company answering their own need to feel good about themselves—and addressing their worst fears about what the consultant might do—the managers could have been prolonging the consultant's suffering. The consultant says that he'd already been diagnosed with pancreatitis, which was, according to him, "a direct result of excessive alcohol abuse." A relapse into drinking could have made this condition worse.

But then again, it's not unusual for seasoned managers to ignore expert advice and abide by their own instincts. It's around such behavior that legendary tales of business prowess are built. But on the flip side, if the decision turns out to be wrong, the business can suffer harsh consequences. In the situation like the one involving the alcoholism of an employee, however, the outcome could have a more severe effect on that employee than it would on the business. That alone ought to be factored into the decision-making process.

But even the best-hearted company managers can't help thinking of the tangible rewards that might result from any investment. This CEO admits as much when he refers to the consultant as "a lucky son of a bitch. We have one very loyal employee." The CEO's convinced that his support for the employee at a time when he was in trouble will translate directly into that employee's loyalty and just possibly make him a more productive worker. Still, no business person, after being hit where it hurts most, the bottom line, is likely to forget that trauma anytime soon. The incident has staying power and can color your attitude about that employee in the future. This CEO admits he'll never have as much trust in the employee as he did before.

It's been nearly a year since the last incident and, says the CEO, "so far, so good. The problem is if he misses a plane or a plane's late, I'm always going to wonder." It turns out that his worries might be justified. Months after the second incident, the employee, who is very candid about his struggle with alcoholism, still seems like he might be in a state of denial, saying he never missed work as a result of his alcoholism. That doesn't bode well for his taking responsibility for his actions. "I wouldn't be surprised if something happened again," says the vice president.

WHEN SELF-INTEREST OUTWEIGHS THE BEST DECISION

For managers who are struggling to make a decision about how far to go to help an employee, it's wise to acknowledge up front whatever degree of self-interest guides your calculations—and to listen carefully to those who know more. The CEO of the computer consulting company, understandably, let his gut instincts lead his thinking and actions. As a result, he never came to terms with whether he truly wanted to do something that would stand the greatest chance of helping the consultant in the long run, even if that meant taking on the guilt associated with giving the consultant his walking papers. The CEO needed to figure out what was best for the company or for the individual employee rather than figure out what actions would make him feel better about himself.

This CEO is a good guy. It's not as if he sat down and calculated how to extract the most from the consultant in his time of need. There's a mix, however, of compassion and selfishness in his decision making that he didn't fully explore. "Business is easy compared to life," he says. "We're just laymen with good hearts and crossed fingers."

Well put. But even so, when faced with such a quandary, company leaders should ask themselves whether their actions are truly designed to help the employee and the company or if they're really just looking to get out of the situation feeling better about themselves. If the latter rings true, they should set aside their own needs. Only then can they begin to weigh their decision about whether the action they want to take to help a troubled employee will truly have a chance of doing just that.

6

Doing the Right
Thing for Legal Reasons

I talk to a lot of people in business—owners, managers, employees, independent contractors—about how they go about making ethical decisions. In larger companies, I'm told about ethical compliance departments, typically made up at least in part of lawyers who help set policies to ensure that the company doesn't violate any laws. One federal government employee told me that whenever the "ethics question" is raised at his agency when they're in the process of making a decision, it's automatically kicked upstairs to the lawyers to figure out. And at smaller companies too, when it comes to ethical decisions about behavior, all too frequently the decision comes down to one based on how to minimize corporate exposure to litigation.

You can see this at work on a day-to-day basis in business when managers forego following what their own best instincts as seasoned businesspeople, and just plain people, tell them to do because they've gotten the message that what their very fiber tells them is right be-havior could possibly expose the company to litigation. In this chap-ter, we look at how such behavior has played itself out in three very distinct areas involving people we work with—firing employees, giv-ing references, and allowing coworkers to be romantically involved.

These are but three of the ways that fear of litigation drives how you make what should be an ethical decision. Next time you're stand-ing around the coffee pot with your coworkers, do a simple test and see how many more examples you can name. The list is endless. Time and again, you see a shoddy business practice that resulted because a manager or employee has acted out of fear of litigation rather than sound business instincts.

That's a sad turn of events. Partly, because the cynic in each of us hardly believes that lawyers are the best source of ethical standards in our society, let alone our business. Funny isn't it, that regardless of the plethora of pejorative jokes about lawyers (and Shakespeare's oft-quoted "kill all the lawyers" line), they're still the ones we turn to in times of making tough ethical choices.

The end result of this fear of litigation is that managers find them-selves being relieved from having to think through difficult decisions. Unfortunately, even in companies that have written ethics compliance policies, such behavior can undermine the credibility of these pro-grams. In a survey of 10,000 randomly selected employees at all levels in six large American companies from a variety of industries, Linda Klebe Trevino, Gary R. Weaver, David G. Gibson, and Barbara Ley Toffler found that "Unless these programs have an impact on everyday decision-making effectiveness, they are not a good use of resources."[1]

The authors of the survey found that: "One of the ways ethics and values get 'baked into' the corporate culture is to make these sorts of discussions the norm." But how can we expect managers to be able to engage in ethical decision making as part of their normal behavior, if every time a tough ethical question comes up, rather than explore it themselves, they automatically kick it upstairs to legal? "In our study," the survey authors continue, "perceptions that ethics is talked about and integrated into decision making were important for all outcomes."

While abdicating responsibility for making ethical decisions may have become standard operating procedure at some companies, in the long-run that does nothing to give employees a sense that its managers are truly able to make these choices either. What's more, a policy of kicking the tough questions up to legal doesn't equip managers to make the black-and-white decisions—let alone those in the gray area. Managers simply fall out of practice. "Ethics codes can be helpful, though not decisive," observe Joseph L. Badaracco, Jr. and Allen P. Web, in their essay "Business Ethics: A View from the Trenches," "particularly if they are specific about acceptable and unacceptable behavior and provide advice on handling 'gray area' matters."[2]

Granted, we make dozens of smaller scale decisions every day that have ethical components to them, but for a good number of management decisions, the fear of litigation has forced the choice out of the hands of seasoned managers directly dealing with employees and the situations that arise, and into the hands of legal or human resources departments. The frightening result may be a generation of managers who are less practiced at decision-making and more seasoned at routing decisions along to the person who can protect the company from exposure.

"By exiling human judgment in the last few decades, modern law changed its role from useful tool to brainless tyrant,"[3] lawyer Philip K. Howard observed in his provocative 1994 book, *The Death of Common Sense: How Law Is Suffocating America.*

Ultimately, the problem with giving way to the brainless tyranny of the law, as Howard sees it is that the "rules, procedures, and rights smothering us are different aspects of a legal technique that promises a permanent fix for human frailty. Dictates are so precise that no one has the chance to think for himself. Procedural layers do away with individual responsibility. Rights are absolute so that choices among conflicting groups never need to be addressed, much less balanced. Law will be cleansed of human input. All tough choices, and indeed all choices, must be predetermined. As citizens and officials, we are allowed to argue during the lawmaking stage, but, day to day, we are precluded from making sense of the problems before us."[4]

But while laws can certainly be very good guides for civil behavior, using them as an automatic tool to relieve oneself from the responsibility of making tough calls in business or life does nothing to increase a person's understanding of why he or she is making the decision. "When humans are not allowed to make sense of the situation," observes Howard, "almost nothing works properly."[5] True enough.

Take the example of making decisions about worker safety. While clearly it makes sense to have laws to protect employees from egregious circumstances that place them in danger, rather than turn first to the manual, you'd think a seasoned manager could think through the challenges presented by the problem and articulate some solutions. The process that manager would have gone through in making those choices is also an important part of the ethical decision making process. Plus, what does it say about managers, when all they do is work from checklists rather than supplement those checklists with their own initiative, ingenuity, concerns, and ideas?

"Freedom depends at least as much on deciding how to do things as on deciding what to do," writes Howard. "Thousands of rigid rules are not needed to satisfy the important goal of worker safety; people could come up with their own plan."[6]

I'm not advocating anarchy in the workplace. The law is, of course, a very necessary thing for society to function well and to protect it from being subjugated by those in power. But relegating every decision to a checklist of rules and regulations rather than relying on your own sense of right and wrong—your own sense of good business practices—can result in a workforce that's incapable of acting as if it were being dictated over by a powerful tyrant.

JUST TRY TO GET A CANDID REFERENCE

You can find examples of how managers and employees are hampered by fear of litigation throughout the workplace. The end result is that whereas in the past, managers and employees could make more thoughtful decisions based on their personal knowledge and common sense, now they're limited by what they're lead to believe exposes them to the least chance of being sued.

Take the case of employee references. Invariably anyone who's tried to get a detailed reference on an employee by making a phone call to a former employer has run into the situation where all the employer will give out is name, rank, and serial number.

In fact, most larger businesses have implicit policies about sending all requests for recommendations to the human resources department rather than have the manager who actually worked with the employee make comments. Once those calls are sent to the human resources department, chances are that all they'll comment on are the dates of the employee's employment at the company. According to a survey conducted by the Society for Human Resource Management in July 1998, while 98 percent of the 854 human resources professionals who responded said they regularly give out dates of employment, only 19 percent would give the reason an employee left an employer, 16 percent would discuss an employee's qualifications for a particular job, 13 percent would comment on work habits, and just 8 percent would comment on bizarre or violent behavior.[7]

The fear, spoken and unspoken, is that giving references can only lead to trouble and likely as not will lead to a lawsuit by a former employee who takes issue with what you had to say about them, or even what you failed to say about them.

The truth is that that fear may be groundless. According to C. Patrick Fleenor, a management professor at the Albers School of Business and Economics at Seattle University, "the fear of being sued and losing is not well founded."[8] In a study made by Fleenor along with Peter Arnesen and Marlin Blizinsky involving court decisions and settlements in Washington, Idaho, and Alaska during 1995 and 1996, they turned up no such cases. None.[9] Fleenor also cited a study conducted by Steven L. Willborn and Ramona Paetzold of federal and state court records nationwide from 1965 to 1970 and 1985 to 1990, that found only 16 defamation cases regarding reference checks. In only 4 of these cases, according to the study, did the plaintiffs prevail.[10]

"Part of the reason you don't see so many of these cases, from the plaintiffs perspective is that they're quite difficult to bring," says Scott Rechtschaffen, an employment lawyer in the San Francisco office of Littler Mendelson. "There are real problems of proof."[11]

In spite of this fact, like most employment lawyers, Rechtschaffen's standard advice to employers is: "Give out minimal name, rank, and serial type information." He observes that this applies to giving good references as well as giving bad ones, since if you're only giving neutral references to former employees who were not among the best performance, "you get into the problem of the employee alleging, 'Well, their failure to give me a reference is in and of itself a negative.' "

In fact, sometimes what you don't say can hurt you. In a California case involving a school that neglected to mention to a prospective employer in its letters of recommendation that its former vice principal had been accused of molesting a teen-age student, the California Supreme Court ruled that the referring school could be held liable for that omission after the vice principal had been accused of molesting a 13-year-old girl at his new school. According to a report of the incident, the court said that the new school "reasonably relied on those letters of recommendation" in hiring the principal. The girl who brought the case alleged that the recommendation letter's omission of complaints against the principal "directly led to his hire" and to the molestation she allegedly suffered from the vice principal.[12]

We're rarely in a position in our business lives, however, of having to decide whether or not to recommend child molesters for a job and, if so, what to include or not in the recommendation. The fear of litigation over giving references has resulted in behavior that smacks of a codified minimalist response that penalizes good employees, prospective employers, and doesn't do a whole lot to suggest that we trust the folks who work with us to have the wherewithal to engage in ethical behavior when they do give employee recommendations.

Employment lawyers will tell you that there's nothing untruthful about sticking to name, rank, and serial number. "You can be truthful, you just can't be open and as forthcoming as you would want to be," says Rechtschaffen, if you want to take the "safest course of action."[13]

We certainly don't want to be reckless, but we don't want to abdicate our responsibilities as managers either. Certainly, it's the lawyers job to let us know where we might face possible legal exposure. But it's not the lawyers' role to tell how we should cease acting in ways that make business sense and are perfectly legal. Fear cripples us.

Besides, when push comes to shove, some people, like Jan Walton, founder of Facilitated Learning, a human resources consulting firm in Manhattan, argue that "the reference battle is over because you don't expect to get information any more," we all know that we can still get more than basic information on prospective employees if we really want to.

But it may not be easy. Dr. Pierre Mornell, a psychiatrist and consultant on hiring to many corporations says that to get a reference on an employee in today's fearful environment, "you have to build a very Rashomon kind of convoluted Byzantine structure."[14]

In his book, *45 Effective Ways for Hiring Smart,* Dr. Mornell suggests one such convolution that seems to work. "Call the references at what you assume will be their lunchtime," he writes, "you want to reach an assistant or voice mail. If it's voice mail, leave a simple message. If it's an assistant, be sure that he or she understands the last sentence of your message. You say: 'John (or Jane) Jones is a candidate for (the position) in our company. Your name has been given as a reference. *Please call me back if that candidate was outstanding.* The results are both immediate and revealing. If the candidate is outstanding or excellent, I guarantee that eight out of ten people will respond quickly and want to help."[15]

But Dr. Mornell acknowledges that you can still get references if you know who should be asking what of whom. "If a lawyer or H.R. person calls a manager or CEO about somebody, they're not going to say anything," he says. "But they will talk back-door with somebody at their own level whom they know."[16]

Employment lawyers talk about this as the "wink-wink, nudge-nudge" behavior that goes on regularly when getting frank recommendations. One former head of personnel for a northern California company with more than 5,000 employees told me as much when he said: "While our company's policy was name, rank, and serial number, off-the-record references were given all the time."

The problem with all this wink-winking and nudge-nudging is that it makes the vast majority of references you get untrustworthy since you never know if the giver of the reference is withholding information or being forthright in talking about an employee. As an employee you can't count on your reputation—good or bad—following you from job to job anymore. And as a manager, it's a crapshoot. You fear giving out frank references and you suspect that you're not getting them either.

According to the *Human Resources Report,* "spurred on by employers' interest in having enough information to make good hires," at least a dozen states are considering "laws that give immunity to employers that provide accurate references for current or former employees."[17] Given the fear of being sued over references, that may come as a welcome sign. But given that we've already allowed lawyers and human resources departments to take over making decisions about what to say about a current or former employee when we're asked for a recommendation, isn't government regulation just another step that takes the responsibility for making reasonable decisions further out of your own hands?

More than $5 billion was spent on employment-law-related training in 1995 and Littler Mendelson projects that companies in the United States will spend $10 billion a year on this area by the year 2000.[18] If indeed the big concern is that managers don't have the training to give appropriate references that don't run afoul of the law, it would seem that a hefty chunk of that money might be better spent going toward training managers and restoring some faith that they're capable of making sound choices when it comes to doling out employee recommendations.

That's not to say that if you're malicious, retaliatory, or express bias about a particular protected class that you won't land in trouble. But c'mon, who doesn't know that if you behave in such a manner, you likely deserve whatever trouble is heaped your way?

The point is that taking that decision-making ability out of the hands of the folks who are best equipped to do the job (the ones who actually worked with the person) runs a serious risk of institutionalizing unthinking behavior. We make tough decisions all day in business. Why take this one away out of fear that somewhere down the line someone might sue the company for something that possibly might be said about someone? Chances are, if that person wants to sue, that person's going to sue regardless of who does the talking.

FEAR OF FIRING

Even *talking* about sensitive issues is something that fear of litigation has put the kabash on in the office. It's not rare these days to walk into your workplace and, as the day goes on, realize that the person who shared the cubicle space next to you for years isn't there anymore. It's not just that he hasn't come into work. All trace of him is nonexistent—the family photos, the potted plants, the cryptic cartoons he liked to clip and post. Gone. As the day goes on, office scuttlebutt has it that he's been canned, shown the big revolving door to the wide-open cruel world. But the funny thing is that no official word—no memo, no department e-mail, nothing—has been issued on what happened to the guy or why he's no longer with the company. He's just gone.

That's the tenor of today's workplace and it's also a casualty wrought by fear of litigation. Companies are so concerned about facing wrongful termination suits that a stunning silence often takes the place of honest and direct communication.

The ethical dilemma that any manager faces today is whether to discipline and fire employees when appropriate and let remaining employees know why these people have been fired so they're clear on what's expected of them, or to build as fortified a wall of silence as possible around any employee termination. The consequences of the first action are obvious: You risk the possibility of being sued by the former employee for what might be construed as defamation. The consequences of the second action may be more subtle, but they're no less serious: Since the remaining workers are unclear on the reasons for your decision to fire someone, you risk creating an environment in which those employees view you as the enemy, someone to be feared, or, at best, not to be trusted. The question then comes down to: What kind of person do you want to be?

Unlike the small number of suits brought over bad recommendations, the number of wrongful termination suits has been exploding over the past several years. So it might be understandable why companies have decided to opt for the silent route. In 1997 alone, more than 24,000 wrongful termination suits were filed, up from 10,000 in 1990, according to David Condon, a lawyer with Edgewater Holdings, an insurer in Chicago.[19]

The proliferation of wrongful termination lawsuits has resulted in employers being scared to offend any group and scared of being sued for defaming a former employee if they reveal any information about the circumstances of a termination. And employees are left mystified and angry when they don't really know what's happened to result in an employee's termination from the organization.

"You want people to understand what the rules are, what standards they and everyone else are being held to," says Michael Daigneault, president of the Washington, DC-based Ethics Resource Center, "In the long run, that not only creates a more disciplined workplace, but also one that's inherently fairer and more just."[20]

But that's simply not happening. And where's the justice in creating an environment where managers are afraid to manage and employees dread coming to work to see who the next unexplained casualty might be?

"The upshot," says Walter K. Olson, senior fellow at the Manhattan Institute and author of *The Excuse Factory: How Employment Law Is Paralyzing the American Workplace,* "is you get a workplace where the law has made speech dangerous. You get something of the loose lips sink ships atmosphere found in wartime. It is the nonmilitary, domestic equivalent of war."[21]

The difference is that in wartime, you can keep morale up by rallying around a crusade against a common enemy. In a company, it's tough going to convince workers that they're in with management on any crusade. So everyone clams up and is left to wonder: What happened to that guy next to me? Or worse, am I next? What does it take to get fired around here anyway?

From the silence around them, employees have few clues. One casualty of such a silent battlefield was Paul J. McCarthy, who was dismissed in January 1994 by a Rochester division of Unisource Worldwide, a big marketer and distributor of paper and packaging systems. For almost four years, McCarthy had worked for a Rochester, New York–based division selling packaging machinery. His termination letter didn't state a reason for the termination, but subsequent correspondence between the company and McCarthy indicated he was let go for "performance-related criteria," a charge McCarthy had been trying for more than four years to get the company to define and one which he adamantly disputes.

McCarthy claims, and others involved concur, that he was fired because he reported an unsavory activity that another employee at Unisource had committed while he was on a sales call with a vendor.[22] The vendor didn't report the incident to Unisource. "We sold over a million dollars worth of product through his company," the vendor explains. "I didn't want to risk losing the business."[23]

But the vendor did tell Paul McCarthy, with whom he'd been friends for a long time, about it. "He went ballistic on it," the vendor says. "Paul's a pretty righteous person and he said, 'this just isn't right. It should be told.'" So McCarthy reported the incident to the regional vice president. That "tattletaling" lead the regional vice president to tell McCarthy's boss to fire him, according to McCarthy and others involved.

The fact though is that since McCarthy was a 39-year-old white male without an employment contract at the time of the firing, and he wasn't part of any protected class or subject to antiretaliation provisions of federal or state whistleblowing statutes, Unisource really didn't need to give a reason for firing him, because of the very aggressive adherence to the concept of "employment at will" in New York State.

When McCarthy was fired from the company, no reason was ever given for his dismissal to the remaining employees, not even those who'd worked with him for years at the Rochester branch. So when he was terminated, he simply amounted to one fewer of the roughly 14,000 people who now report to work at Unisource Worldwide every day.

Patrick Farris, senior counsel at Unisource Worldwide's headquarters in Berwyn, Pennsylvania, said, "The company is very comfortable with the decision that it made with respect to his termination."[24]

By all accounts, Paul McCarthy very likely didn't have a lawsuit he could bring and he knew it. If anything he was a victim of a company trying hard to follow its policies in an environment heavily laden with the threat of employee lawsuits. The company certainly didn't want to do anything to increase its chances of giving McCarthy something to sue about. And one way to do that is to remain silent.

Where's the ethical issue in all of this? It's simple. The fear of getting sued has resulted in companies being full of people who are afraid of leveling with one another about the real issues surrounding performance or termination, afraid to do their jobs, afraid to talk with one another, which doesn't exactly lay the groundwork for a well-managed workforce.

Because of this fear of litigation, says Mary Dollarhide, a labor lawyer with Paul, Hastings, Janofsky & Walker in Stamford, Connecticut, "there are managers who simply refuse to manage. It's a practice that's likely to backfire. Let's say you've got somebody in a protected class and, for reasons having nothing to do with their skin color, they're just a lousy performer. You don't counsel them because you're afraid you're going to get stuck with some bogus lawsuit having to do with their protected status. When things deteriorate to where you have to fire this person, you're going to end up with an empty personnel file without a lick of evidence that anything was ever wrong. And they're going to be sitting in front of a jury saying 'Hey, my manager never said anything to me about needing to improve my performance.' I've got lots of lawsuits like that."[25]

The fear of getting sued quite simply has forced people to treat one another badly. They don't talk, or when they do talk they don't say anything. At large companies, where the distance between the employee and the folks he's dealing with is greater, the matter becomes all the more impersonal.

When using reasonable and fair judgment to make a decision gives way to relying on the expediency of what the law allows or the fear of litigation dictates, there aren't a lot of winners in the workplace. Sure, it's safe, but again it's a further indication that rather than be allowed to make decisions based on thoughtful, intelligent reflection (behavior we'd like to think the managers and employees working for our company are capable of), we're letting fear of litigation drive our choices. The thinking goes out of the equation.

So what about Paul McCarthy? When asked about the reasons for McCarthy's termination and lack of a clear reason ever given for why he was fired, Patrick Farris, senior counsel at Unisource Worldwide's headquarters in Berwyn, Pennsylvania, says: "The company, our company, doesn't typically discuss personnel or employee issues for a number of reasons that I am sure you can appreciate, issues of confidentiality and the like." The termination, he says, was "performance-related." When asked to define "performance-related" Farris responded, "I think the statement speaks for itself."[26]

Hmm. The funny thing is that when the policy is not to speak at all, perhaps it's hard for the silence not to speak for itself as well.

So sometimes, as in the case of dismissed employees, fear of litigation results in a lack of thoughtful discourse about what's going on. Employees may be left in the dark about what really is expected of them and managers may be handcuffed because they feel they can't discuss the recent dismissal in even the broadest of terms.

That shouldn't be the case. For one thing it sends an unclear message to your workforce. They might wonder whether firing is an arbitrary process at your company. It begs the question: Why was this person let go? And, from a management standpoint, it rids you of an opportunity not only to reassure employees who are doing good jobs, but also to make clear what is expected of them. Perhaps doing this without speaking ill of the person fired is difficult, but it's hardly impossible. And being open about the circumstances, talking it through with employees, is worth the effort. Sure it takes time, but so too do all those hours of lost productivity due to employees gossiping about the issue or feeling stymied because the message you've sent them is so ambiguous they question their own ability to do their job.

RELATIONSHIPS IN THE WORKPLACE

But sometimes fear of litigation has the almost opposite effect on behavior in the workplace. When businesses fear that not talking about something may lead to a lawsuit, they find themselves in the oddest of discussions.

Consider how consensual relationships in the workplace are now treated. A wonderful byproduct of Anita Hill's allegations of sexual harassment in her 1991 testimony in the Clarence Thomas Supreme Court nomination hearings before the Senate judiciary committee was that companies grew more aware that sexual harassment was an issue they should pay serious attention to in the workplace. Protecting a woman or a man's right to work in a nonhostile environment is certainly a noble enough effort. And educating managers who might not have been quite so enlightened about inappropriate behavior in the workplace certainly could have created some thoughtful discussions about the importance of treating fellow employees with respect.

But when that concern shifts primarily from the welfare of the worker to focus more on whether the company is going to be held legally liable for allowing such actions to occur, the result once again can lead to behavior designed primarily to avoid lawsuits. In the case of sexual harassment, the trouble is that as a result of being overly fearful of litigation, companies can enact policies that not only attempt to stave off the flow of sexual harassment in the workplace, but also nip in the bud any consensual behavior that might possibly lead to sexual harassment down the road. So rather than have a discussion with employees over inappropriate behavior and admonish employees who step over the line, the discussion shifts to a Twilight-zone-like, how-can-we-stop-even-the-remotest-possibility-of-this-type-of-behavior-happening-ever approach, where nothing is left up to the individual employees' integrity or ability to discern appropriate behavior. As a result, the treatment and policies surrounding how to prevent inappropriate relationships in the workplace are wildly inconsistent.

At the height of the Clinton impeachment hearings, and throughout the year leading up to it, there was a wide cry that any CEO found to be having a consensual sexual relationship with a young intern or staff member would have been shown the door as fast as all get out.[27] Well, that's not true.

Carol Sanger, a professor of law at Columbia Law School, who teaches courses on sex discrimination and family law, confirmed that: "In the cases that I've been reading, that's just not so."[28]

That's not to say that when incidents of blatant sexual harassment do occur in the workplace, companies are not doing the right thing and taking a strong stance against the person doing the harassing. It's when you start looking at how companies have dealt with the issue of "inappropriate relationships" in the workplace that it seems as if many companies have not thoughtfully addressed the issue.

As it turns out, most companies have no written policies about workplace romance. In a survey taken of 600 human resource professionals in January 1998 by the Society for Human Resource Management, 72 percent of them said their company had no written or unwritten policy on workplace romances. Of those businesses that did have a policy, more than half of them said that it discouraged, but didn't forbid office romances completely. When asked, the human resources professionals said that the most likely outcome of a romance in their company was marriage.[29]

If company owners, managers, CEOs, boards of directors, and human resources professionals wanted to face the real ethical issue underlying workplace relationships, they shouldn't focus on whether or not a CEO who dates an employee who is half his age should be fired. Instead, they should address the question of what effect this behavior has on the company, and just as importantly, what effect does it have on the rest of the employees?

The real challenge of a policy on workplace romances is not to avoid potential lawsuits or decide the appropriate age gap between consenting adults, but rather to look at how to address workplace romances so that all parties can be dealt with humanely; how companies can insure that any behavior that might be consensual and condoned by the company doesn't jeopardize the professional careers of other people at the company; and how companies can keep employees from using their position and power to entice other employees (of lesser power and position) into relationships they do not want.

Unfortunately, most companies view the problem as a liability issue rather than as an ethical issue. Rather than address the challenges above, the goal shifts to how the company can avoid any sexual harassment lawsuits that come about as a result of a workplace relationship that ends badly or from those employees who feel like they're discriminated against because they would not engage in a relationship with a higher-up.

Nancy E. Pritikin, a partner in the San Francisco office of Littler Mendelson, an employment law firm, has worked on issues of sexual harassment in the workplace. She recognizes the problem of companies doing whatever they can to avoid lawsuits. "We live in such a litigious society, where people are so willing to make claims," she says. "And the claims are so expensive to deal with—even when you win them—that companies are really struggling with ways to avoid the problem."[30]

Over the past several years, some companies that don't have a policy against workplace relationships now require that the person who has the higher ranking position in the company disclose that relationship to the company's human resources department. Both parties then meet with the human resources department and are asked to sign a contract that acknowledges their consent to the relationship and frees the company of any liability. These have become known as "love forms," or "love contracts" and while they might suggest that companies have begun to deal with a difficult issue in the workplace, they do seem a ridiculous way to treat adults.[31]

Writing thoughtful policies about sexual harassment in the workplace is fairly straightforward. The bottom line is that most reasonable people agree that sexual harassment is bad and should not be tolerated in the workplace. But workplace romance doesn't necessarily automatically add up to sexual harassment, so the issue of how to think about such behavior in the workplace gets really hazy.

"I don't know whether our society is prepared to take the step of saying you cannot date anyone you work with," Ms. Pritikin says. "But disclosure is one step in the right direction for the manager, company and individual, so they can be sure that no one's being taken advantage of. Sure, we're talking about pretty private behavior here. But when you're a manager or a supervisor, you can't expect that you can have a completely private relationship with a person at work who reports to you."[32]

Professor Sanger of Columbia observed that when it comes to workplace romances: "No one knows quite what to do. But it's ridiculous to think that people at work aren't going to fall in love."[33]

Since we spend most of our waking hours in the workplace, that's a decidedly obvious, yet very true observation. But companies have the challenge of deciding whether it's appropriate for them to have any role in letting coworkers fall in love and, if so, what that role will be.

FEARS CAN BE BLINDING

If your actions in the workplace are to be based solely on a fear of lit-igation, then sadly the end result is a policy that is less than likely to address human needs and concerns in the workplace. Instead, it'll be operated out of a liability management mindset. And since no rules can predict the nuance of individual circumstance, the law drives what should have been a thoughtful discussion into a rigid set of instructions.

"In a system of final rules, every decision is a binary choice," Philip K. Howard wrote in *The Death of Common Sense*. "Yes or no, legal or illegal, proper procedure or Return to Go, we are constantly poked by legal dictates that keep us in our predetermined place. 'The rule of joy and the law of duty,' Holmes once observed, 'seem to me all one.' Today, we have lost our joy, and much more, because modern law tells us our duty is only to comply, not to accomplish. Understanding of the situation has been replaced by legal absolutism."[34]

We make decisions every day in business that require ethical re-flection—choices ranging from which one of a group of equally qual-ified candidates to hire and what kind of payment schedule to use with vendors, to how much information to disclose to employees about the financial condition of the company, and how to fire an underper-forming employee. Sure, sometimes the decisions are more complex than others, but they're all difficult decisions that require careful thought about what the outcome might be for the various constituents involved.

If we give over this process to relying on a rigid set of rules de-signed to protect us from getting sued, we risk losing control of doing what we can to work in the type of business we want to work in. Ab-staining from responsibility for making tough choices by using the fear of litigation as a crutch is no real solution since we end up making de-cisions that might indeed have good outcomes (or might have bad ones) without really knowing why we made this decision other than the fact that someone somewhere decided that's the way it's done to avoid exposure.

As employment lawyer Mary Dollarhide observed, the risk of letting ourselves be guided by a set of checklists and rules without thinking about what's behind our actions when we make choices in the workplace is that we end up with "managers who simply refuse to manage" because they're afraid of getting "stuck with some bogus lawsuit."[35]

Certainly, it's easier to rely blindly on a set of legal rules and checklists rather than thinking through the implications of each specific decision that needs to be made. But then we end up with companies full of managers who refuse to manage, who refuse to take personal responsibility for thinking through their decisions. That's hardly a sound foundation on which to build a company.

What magnifies the problem is that as avoiding exposure becomes a bigger and bigger part of our jobs, we run the risk of being consumed not only by keeping track of all the things we can't do for fear of lawsuits, but also by losing sight of what we really think as participants in the workplace about what is the right thing to do.

7

❀

Where Do We
Draw the Lines?

M y father worked most of his adult life for the federal government. He was an agronomist with the Soil Conservation
Service, which was a division of the U.S. Department of
Agriculture. For as long as I can remember, his job involved field
work. Part of his responsibility was to use aerial photographs to map
the particular soils that existed in a given area. When a particular
county or region was completely mapped, a team would write up a report based on its findings and then move on to the next county. The
result was to give those who planned to use the land a guide to what
soils and terrain existed in any given region of the country.

Don't worry. I haven't shifted topics into the arcane world of agron-
omy that only those trained to read aerial photographs, recognize and
test various soils, and carry into the field with them medieval-looking

soil augurs would find of interest. I bring this up because as a federal government employee, my father's world of work was far different from my world of work and that of many of you who are reading this book.

In his work, the expectations for the job were clearly proscribed. I can still remember the tiny card he carried around that listed all the grade levels and steps within those grade levels that dictated what salary he might expect as he moved up in the SCS. His goals were set at the outset of the project and he could navigate pretty clearly between the lines of his work world and his personal life. While he occasionally socialized with some of his coworkers and he sometimes brought work home, the line between his role as an employee of the federal government and a private individual with a family were pretty clear.

For better or worse, for a growing number of people these days those lines are not as clear. Some of this has to do with the changing nature of work, particularly in the private sector. As more women have entered the workforce, family responsibilities change so more flexible work hours are provided for many men and women. Some companies are experimenting with letting employees set their own hours with clear expectations of productivity goals laid out ahead of time.

Advances in technology have also blurred the lines for people. Even for those employees and managers who don't telecommute, the advent of e-mail and the rapid development of the Internet have made it possible to stay wired to the office even when you're not in the office. When we're on the road for business or on our own personal time, many of us can use our laptops or home computers to dial the office computer server and download any e-mail we might have received while we were out. And the number of people who have this capability continues to mushroom. Between January and August 1998 alone, the number of PCs connected to the Internet in the United States increased by 35 percent, from 45 million to more than 60 million. According to Ziff-Davis, that means that 53 percent of all PCs in use are now connected to the Internet. The growth in the number of PCs in the workplace that have Internet hookups has been staggering—an increase of 52 percent over the same time period, from 16 million to more than 24 million. What's more, 35 percent of all PCs in the workplace, and 60.4 percent in the home, are connected to the Internet six hours or more per week.[1]

In this chapter, I'll look at some ways in which those blurred boundaries have raised issues that require new ways of thinking about ethical behavior in the workplace. One involves the issue of e-mail privacy that has been brought about by the explosion of the Internet; the other has to do with the advances in medical technology that have allowed for transplants among nonrelatives, something which had been not nearly as successful in past years.

Both of these examples are in highly charged areas with significant ethical issues. But there are countless examples of the blurring between work and personal life—whether it's because we're always reachable by voice or data (no need to wait to get back to the office to call or jot down a message); how our work travel affects our child care needs and options; or how work can determine what kind of medical care we get and which doctors we can use. While I've chosen specific examples in this chapter, the issues they raise (about employee privacy, an employee's relationship to a boss, the need to talk about the implications of the actions that cross boundaries) can be applied to those boundary issues you face every day.

We are indeed one connected nation. That's just part of the reason that the issue of how we distinguish between our personal lives and our business lives grows more murky. It becomes more difficult to clearly separate these two aspects of our lives.

From an ethical standpoint, perhaps some of the murkiness of where our work life stops and our private life begins is to be expected. Over the past several decades, the prevailing thinking that held that the way people behaved in their private lives didn't necessarily have any reflection on how they did or should be expected to behave in their business lives has been shifting. Alfred Carr and Milton Friedman were chief among those propagating that prevailing wisdom. In his article in the September 13, 1970, *New York*

Times Magazine, Friedman took his now well-known position that a business' social responsibility is to its stockholders and therefore, the main objective is to increase the business' profits.[2] In a 1967 article for *The New York Times,* Alfred Carr used a poker analogy to argue that business is a game in which there are certain rules. In a person's business life, Carr would hold, he or she would set aside personal ethics and values in order to meet the needs of the corporation.[3]

But there's been a shift in thinking about whether the notion we can park our personal beliefs at the door when we enter the corporate world is valid. Proponents of virtue ethics believe that it's wrong-headed to think that we can or ever could. Writing in the *Journal of Applied Philosophy,* John Morse observes that "the virtue theorist insists that any ethical decision we make is based on a set of dispositions we have acquired throughout our life. When someone acts unethically in a business transaction, this is bound to break down the good character habit which he or she has developed up to this point. The virtue theorist denies that there is an ability to separate the 'business' self from the 'private' self, because the actions in each realm form dispositions which apply to a person's general manner of acting."[4]

Morse concludes that "Friedman and Carr are wrong, for they try to separate the moral ramifications of actions within a business environment from their effects on the individuals with whom business comes into contact. Business has to be seen as a moral entity which is an integral part of the community, and it must therefore be concerned about the welfare of the community within which it is situated, as well as the welfare of the individuals whom it influences."[5]

As employees, managers, or owners, our actions have an effect on those surrounding us. This is hardly a new notion. Aristotle wrote in *Politics* that each of us is "by nature a political animal" and that "He who is unable to live in society, or who has no need because he is sufficient for himself, must be either a beast or a god."[6]

The challenge is to learn how to live in society and not take an easy out when making decisions that we know, based upon our own values, to be wrong. "Ethics is how we behave when we decide we belong together," write Margaret Wheatley and Myron Kellner-Rogers in their book, *A Simpler Way*. "Daily we see this interplay of ethics and belonging in our own lives. We want to be part of an organization. We observe what is accepted or rewarded and we adapt. But these ethics are not always good. We may agree to behaviors that go against personal or societal values. Months or years later, we dislike the person we have become. Did we sacrifice some essential aspect of ourself in order to stay with an organization? What was the price of belonging?"[7]

That challenge to stay true to personal values and still survive within an organization is certainly heightened as the boundaries between work and personal life get blurred. "Managing our boundaries leads to questions about necessary tensions," Alan Briskin observes in *The Stirring of Soul in the Workplace*. He continues:

> The boundary questions about authority ask: How do we lead but remain open to criticism? How do we follow but still challenge superiors? The boundary questions involving task are: How do we depend on others we don't control? How do we specialize yet understand other people's jobs? Questions about power involve personal reward: What's in it for us? And questions about identity involve differentiation from others: Who is—and who isn't—us? The tensions raised by these questions involved defending one's interests without undermining the organization and feeling pride without devaluing others. . . . The discipline of taking these questions seriously changes the nature of viewing the organization as simply a place of domination and submission, or inclusion and exclusion, and substitutes a personal responsibility for managing one's own boundaries in relation to others. These questions obligate us simultaneously to respect our own subjective experience and still attend to others. The result, if pursued, is a greater permeability between self and others and between self and work.[8]

But this permeability that we're trying to manage is often fraught with conflicts, sometimes in ways that on the surface might seem pedestrian in nature. Take the issue of how the proliferation of e-mail and Internet use in the workplace has had an impact on the relationship between employer and employee.

E-MAIL CHANGES EVERYTHING

Most of us in our work lives from time to time have performed personal tasks while on the job. Because our lives are so involved, it's nearly impossible not to take time during work to place a telephone call to check in with our child's caretaker or to place a call to a friend to confirm an evening's plans. And most of us, over the years, have assumed that our personal telephone calls—as long as we didn't abuse the practice and spend the bulk of our working hours on personal matters—would remain private. Oh sure, occasionally an employer might speak with us if they noticed our long-distance calls were aberrantly large during a given time period, but mostly the issue of privacy was respected.

Along comes e-mail, which for many has replaced the phone call as the quick contact method of choice. The trouble is that what we might have said in an unrecorded phone call now becomes documented in writing on a system that is owned by our employer. What's more, for many of us, our work e-mail address is our *only* e-mail address, so we use it to correspond with professional contacts, but also with personal contacts. And because it seems less formal than a letter or memo, we aren't always particularly self-editing when it comes to composing an e-mail missive.

And that leads to all kinds of issues from the troublesome ones over what kind of privacy can an employee expect from his or her employer to what kind of legal exposure is the employer subject to if he or she doesn't set some guidelines for e-mail usage. The mistakes are regularly recounted by word-of-mouth ("Oops, didn't mean to copy *you* on *that.*") as well as tales in the press about e-mail messages gone awry. In one case reported in *The Wall Street Journal,* the story was told of Anthony Butler, a pharmaceuticals analyst at

Lehman Brothers. As it happens, Butler sent an e-mail about a colleague to an investment banker at Lehman. The colleague was being wooed by a Lehman competitor and Butler wrote that he "is making a mistake" and "forgot how much we at Lehman created and allowed him to accomplish."[9] Mr. Butler also added that he would gladly assume his colleague's duties.

The problem was that just after sending the message out, Butler apparently realized that rather than sending the e-mail to the Lehman investment banker, he'd sent it to 75 of Lehman's money-manager clients at mutual funds, insurance companies, and banks. After he realized what he had done, he sent off a second message asking the unintended receivers to disregard the initial message. *The Wall Street Journal* quoted Butler as saying, "I'm technologically an idiot, to put it candidly. I still don't understand what happened, or even how it happened." But in spite of the embarrassment it caused Mr. Butler, all turned out well for him since eventually his colleague left Lehman and Butler did seem likely to take over some of his duties.

It doesn't always turn out so well for the e-mail writer who doesn't think carefully about the impact of what he or she is writing and how writing the e-mail creates a permanent document that can be retrieved long after it has left the sender's computer. In a case involving Nissan in California, two female employees were fired after a supervisor read e-mail they'd been sending to one another in which they commented on the supervisor's sexual prowess. He fired the women. They sued and lost.[10]

On another occasion, Beth Gunn and Alec Myers, two workers at Opta Food Ingredients, a food science company in Bedford, Massachusetts, were fired after a practical joke they pulled went awry and their boss read their e-mail. The terms they'd used to refer to him were none too positive, including: "old bald-headed goat," "idiot," "useless control freak pseudo figurehead numbskull," among others.[11] They'd written a fake ransom note involving mulch they'd collected from the company parking lot and a fellow employee intercepted the note and turned it over to the CEO. He called Gunn and Myers into his office to announce that he would be conducting an investigation. He found not only the unflattering references to himself, but also a whole series of sardonically written e-mail messages that had been sent between Gunn and Myers including those that joked about planting drugs on a fellow employee and bombing the building. The CEO fired them both for misconduct and refused to pay them unemployment benefits. A two-year unemployment court battle followed that eventually resulted in Gunn and Myers receiving unemployment benefits for the time they were unemployed. Gunn and Myers ultimately decided to attend law school.[12]

Similar cases have occurred throughout the country. And the outcome is generally that the courts are finding that the employer has the right to eavesdrop on an employee's e-mail, in part because the company owns the system on which the e-mail is sent typically on company time. The real question employers have to ask themselves is whether simply having the right to monitor and read their employees' e-mail makes it something they want to do. It is an invasion of privacy, legal or not, and how employers decide to handle the policing of e-mail within their companies will send a distinct message to employees about how much they trust them.

Does the e-mail being sent by employees pose enough of a risk in lost productivity or exposure to litigation to justify an employer's subjecting e-mail to monitoring? And employees have to ask themselves if their concern is really over what some suggest is an invasion of their constitutional rights to privacy or if they simply don't want to get caught with all those e-mails they've been sending on company time to online auction houses or large Internet booksellers, or worse, all those e-mails in which they've referred to their boss as a weasel.

With International Data Corporation estimating that in the year 2000, 90 million workers in the United States will send 2.8 billion e-mail messages a day,[13] the issue of how companies monitor their e-mail systems is only going to get more complicated. Employees may argue that it's an invasion of privacy, but companies can also argue that if they don't monitor the e-mail that's going out over their systems, they end up exposing themselves not just to internal problems involving employee misconduct, but also to outside forces.

Since most companies store backup copies of every e-mail sent out on its system, if they find themselves in a lawsuit, the suing company can subpoena years worth of a company's e-mail. If any damaging comments are made internally, they can be used in a court case. Regardless of who wins the case, the result can be an incredible distraction and sapping of time for a company, plus facing the embarrassment of what might have been composed as off-the-cuff remarks surfacing in a trial.

In one such case, a company brought suit against another claiming that an employee at the company being sued had undermined a project that they had been working on together by bad-mouthing the plaintiff. The company being sued turned over e-mail dealing with the project. That employee cited as undermining the project was referred to as a "loose cannon" by a fellow employee.[14] While the plaintiff was originally awarded damages in the case, that verdict was overturned. In spite of that vindication, that loose cannon reference became widely known to all the parties involved and couldn't have helped but cause embarrassment for the company.

Margaret Wheatley and Myron Kellner-Rogers wisely observe that:

> Large organizations spend a great deal of time and resources on training people in behaviors under such topics as diversity, communications, and leadership. But these behaviors are not a list of rules or techniques. They arise from agreements about how people will be together. Often these agreements are unspoken. We can't train people to be open, or fair, or responsible if the real agreement is that we must succeed at all costs, or that we have no choice but to keep laying people off. Training programs can never resolve deeply incoherent messages. Neither can legislation. Behaviors are rooted in our agreements. They change only when we bring to light these unspoken commitments. Our behaviors change only if we decide to belong together differently.[15]

Wheatley and Kellner-Rogers' observation that many of the agreements we have about what type of behavior is acceptable are unspoken but understood is a noble thought. The problem is that there's only so much ambiguity we can expect an employee to be able to understand and interpret into acceptable behavior. With new technologies being advanced in the workplace at a rapid pace, some of these previously unspoken agreements must be talked about and clarified if the employer has any hope of ensuring that employees make good decisions.

No memo from the human resources department is going to help employees understand what's behind their employer's concerns when a policy gets handed down. Because there are a growing number of issues in the workplace that make knowing what is appropriate behavior more difficult (understanding, for example, that what transpires in a phone conversation is highly different from what transpires in an e-mail), employers must find a way to talk to employees to help them sort through the muck. The company that was sued and subpoenaed for its e-mail records might have decided to use that court case as a tool to discuss the importance of how e-mails were written in the workplace. After all, the case is widely posted on the Internet and cited in more than one law journal article. It never did.

JUST TALK ABOUT IT

The trouble is that when it comes to solving business dilemmas within their workplaces most companies don't take the simplest solution: They don't talk about them. Had the company that was sued for the errant e-mail wanted, it could have used the suit as one of the most potent tools available to it to make clear how e-mail conversations differed from phone conversations and why employees might consider more care in how they composed their thoughts using the technology.

Often though, companies just don't talk about issues when they arise. Partly, this results from the difficulty managers might have in airing information that could paint the company or some of its employees in a less than favorable light. It's also all too common for discussions about decisions that involve exploring the various dimensions about what's right and what's wrong in a given situation to be too painful to confront. So instead, employees just muddle through with little guidance or room for discussion.

But as anyone who has spent anytime in the corridors or lunchrooms of companies knows, employees know when something is amiss within a company. If there is not disclosure about what's happened, more inventive alternatives are imagined. The result provides little in the way of helping employees or managers find a way to thoughtfully examine their actions.

This silence as standard operating procedure when it comes to uncomfortable situations is endemic even in companies that are inherently open with their employees. Some situations, some conundrums, just don't seem right to discuss. That poses a problem since it can leave employees confused about what's appropriate or what's expected. Employers may think that "of course, our employees understand the implications of this action," but often as not they don't. And if no discussion has taken place within the workplace, why would you expect them to?

I took a lot of heat not long ago for reporting the story of a very noble act taken by an incredibly courageous woman in her workplace.[16] It was the story of Nancy Nearing, a systems analyst for Applied Management Systems of Rockville, Maryland, and her boss, Art Helms, a software project manager and her supervisor at the same company.

I first read about the story in an article by syndicated columnist Ellen Goodman. "Nancy Nearing gave at the office," Goodman wrote. "And I do not mean the United Way. The 42-year-old Virginia mother of two gave a kidney. To her boss."[17]

But the part of the story that really intrigued me was when I read the portion of an article in *The Washington Post* that said: "All potential donors are given a psychiatric evaluation to make sure their reasons for donating an organ—usually a kidney, but also bone marrow or a piece of a lung or liver—are sound. Because the intended recipient in this case was Nearing's boss, the psychiatrist recommended that she also see an ethicist."[18] I was intrigued by who this "ethicist" might have been and what the experience was like for Ms. Nearing. It was only after reporting the piece that I found that the psychiatrist didn't send Nearing to see an ethicist. (Her surgeon spoke to a member of the ethics board of the hospital where the transplant would occur.) But I grew interested in the fact that conversations that could have happened in the workplace didn't. And I'm not talking here about conversations between Ms. Nearing and Art Helms, the boss to whom she volunteered to donate a kidney.

But some details first. For three-and-a-half years, Mr. Helms had been spending three afternoons a week on dialysis. Doctors then told him in May 1998 that both of his kidneys would have to be removed. Helms told his staff at AMS that after he had the operation, his name would be placed on a waiting list for a donor kidney and that he expected to be out of the office for several weeks while he recuperated.

It was after he'd made the announcement to his staff that Nancy Nearing offered him one of her kidneys. He says he never expected the reaction. "The gesture blew me away," he says.[19]

Mr. Helms says that at first he didn't take Ms. Nearing's offer seriously. But undeterred, she did the necessary research and ultimately it was determined that she was a match as a kidney donor for Mr. Helms.

"I don't think he was prepared for someone bouncing into his hospital room saying, 'Guess what? We can do this,'" she said. "And this was probably the first time I'd ever seen him outside of work."

The question I posed at the time was why, if the two of them weren't close friends, Ms. Nearing, a mother of two who's worked a part-time schedule (she says she works 26 hours a week for the company) since starting with AMS in June of 1995, would make such an offer to the man she reports to at work?

"You have a guy who does all the things you want a boss to do," she says. "He gives you the tools you need to do your job right. He bends over backwards to facilitate whatever schedule you need so that you can actually have a family life. Wouldn't you try to keep it going?"

That strong sense of caring by an individual for a supervisor in the workplace is not unusual. In fact, it's critical to an employee's psyche that he or she not have a sense of fear or ambiguity about his or her boss—if you want that employee to be productive. In *Ethics and Excellence: Cooperation and Integrity in Business,* Robert C. Solomon observes that:

> Caring in the corporation consists of a fundamental attitude. That attitude is one of mutual affection and obligation. This does not mean mawkish sentiments, and it does not suggest that the best executive is one that treats or thinks of his or her employees as children. It does mean that the recognition and treatment of one's employees as people, full of fears and jealousies and other unbusinesslike emotions, is essential to the bonding that corporate life requires. It involves the recognition that a resentful employee is a minimally cooperative and potentially destructive employee, and that a fearful employee—especially if the fear is for his or her job—is an employee who cannot, despite appearances and efforts to the contrary, be expected to be a loyal and dedicated employee. When the tie to one's job becomes evidently contingent, one's devotion to the job becomes cautious, calculated and merely contingent too. And when one is plagued by fears for the future, the threat of sickness or financial ruin, one cannot expect adequate focus on the present or on the job at hand. Executives who see health and retirement benefits simply as a "perk" or, worse, as a wasted but unfortunately necessary expenditure on the future of those who will no longer be productive employees, are greatly missing the point. Caring is not just charity, and it is not represented by selfless generosity. Caring is the unity and the health of any ongoing organization. It is the dynamic of the present as well as an investment in the future.[20]

Clearly, that "mutual affection and obligation" that Solomon speaks of appears to have existed between Mr. Helms and Ms. Nearing. Her remarks suggest that Mr. Helms made the employees in his workplace trust that he cared about them as people, apparently enough so that Ms. Nearing made this more than generous offer.

Ms. Nearing's act is one of great altruism. Between the time he had his kidneys removed on July 14, and the transplant on September 10 when he received one of Ms. Nearing's kidneys, Helms had experienced congestive heart failure twice. Her act helped her boss live. It was an act that one would hardly *expect* from an employee in the normal course of business, even if Mr. Helms' condition was so severe.

There are times, Robert Solomon observes, that the "idea of going *beyond* morality, beyond the call of duty, is nowhere more evident than in those special people whom we designate as *saints* and *heroes*." He defines those saints as "not just someone who is perfectly good in the easy sense of not sinning (perhaps because there have been no opportunities); a saint is extraordinarily good, resisting temptations that we cannot imagine resisting and doing good deeds that are far beyond the demands of duty of charity. Similarly, a hero or heroine is a person who does not do just what is commanded, but much more—indeed, much more than anyone could have expected."[21]

It's not our duty to be a saint or a hero and no one can order us to be saintly or heroic. But, as Solomon concludes, "our ethics would be impoverished without such concepts and if we did not aspire to *be* such persons. This aspiration inspires the best in us and the best of what we call our morals." When we do our duty and feel self-righteous about it, that's altogether different. The saint and the hero typically "do not even think of what they are doing in such terms. Indeed. It is in part that naiveté, devoid of self-doubt and deliberation, that may make them saints and heroes."[22]

In the context of offering to donate a kidney to her boss, Nancy Nearing clearly would seem to fall into this definition of a saint in the workplace.

So where's the ethical issue in all of this? Come back to the issue that there were conversations that could have taken place in the workplace but never did. While Ms. Nearing says she and Mr. Helms discussed the issue of whether the donation would affect Mr. Helms' ability to fire her if he ever had to (she wrote me after the original column appeared to tell me that he assured her that he could[23]), but that was a discussion they had among themselves. No one in the company ever discussed with them or with other employees and managers within the small company how it might affect their relationship in the workplace.

Ms. Nearing obviously cared about Mr. Helms as her boss and wanted to continue the relationship that was working very well. But regardless of how sincere and altruistic her motives were—saintly and heroic even—there is still a dilemma that is implicit in Ms. Nearing's reason for donating her kidney to Mr. Helms. She cares about Mr. Helms as a boss and wants to keep that relationship going. Her generous gift to Mr. Helms—which by all measures can be classified as selfless—went beyond what most would consider traditional workplace boundaries. That's not to say she shouldn't have done it; given its layers of possible interpretation, it would have been a perfect opportunity for the issue to be raised in the workplace.

Ms. Nearing's charitable act raises difficult questions: Could Mr. Helms really ever fire her should the need arise? And how will the transplant affect theirs and other work relationships at the company?

It may seem tacky to even raise such issues. But someone at the company, aside from Ms. Nearing and Mr. Helms (who was, remember, medically indisposed while these donation decisions were being made), might have put the issue on the table by discussing the implications of her actions with the rest of the workforce. It wasn't as if the owner and company administrators didn't know about the act. But no one discussed it. "It never entered my mind," said Margaret Hutchison, the director of administration, whom Ms. Nearing called to arrange for time off to recuperate.

Essentially, the only time the issues came up was during Ms. Nearing's meeting with the psychiatrist that the Georgetown Medical Institute requires donors to see before a transplant. At that meeting, Ms. Nearing was taken aback. "They were really hung up on the fact that he was my manager," she said of the hospital. "It was uncomfortable, and it made me angry."

The company should have discussed the issues with her and with Mr. Helms, says Sharon Daloz Parks, a coauthor of *Common Fire: Leading Lives of Commitment in a Complex World* and associate director of the Whidbey Institute, a career development and spiritual retreat center in Clinton, Washington. "She is doing this in hopes that it preserves continuity in her work life, but if, in the future, she needs to be reviewed for any type of underperformance, who does that?" Ms. Parks asked. "What happens if other workers begin to feel that she is in some way inadequate, but she's forever with us because she gave a kidney to the boss?"

Ms. Parks is hardly being cynical, although some would read her reaction that way. In fact, in *Common Fire,* Ms. Parks and her coauthors observe that it's all too easy these days to dismiss motives like those of Ms. Nearing in a cynical manner:

> In a time of pervasive complexity, cynicism provides the false comfort of the simple conviction that all human motivation can be reduced to narrow self-interest and conflicting autonomous choices. Thus there is little imagination of a collective will, of shared participation and belonging. In a climate of pervasive cynicism, every gesture in the name of the public good is demeaned and every act of generosity dismissed as merely self-serving. 'Enlightened self-interest' becomes the parched and only ground in which hope for the common good must struggle to take root.[24]

But this observation doesn't seem to be indicative of that same cynicism she writes about in her book. Instead, Parks and her coauthors suggest that Ms. Nearing's act raises issues that are unusual for the workplace that should have been addressed but weren't.

And the issues being raised are new. Ten years ago, nonrelated living kidney donations were hardly possible. Today, as waiting lists grow and medical technology improves transplantation success, they've become more prevalent as a possible solution. Since it is such a dramatic, unusual gesture and it takes place between a boss and an employee, wouldn't it make sense for the owner or managers to discuss the issues that might be on every other worker's mind but that they might be reluctant to raise for fear of seeming petty? Even if it turned out to be a non-issue, wouldn't that have partially prepared Ms. Nearing for the meeting with the hospital psychiatrist? Her decision may have been a highly personal one, but when it crossed over into workplace territory, it became one which also had an impact on her colleagues.

Ms. Nearing doesn't believe "that there was any corporate laxity" she told me in an e-mail after I first told the story. "I am proud to work in an organization of professionals where we are all trusted to act as professionals," she wrote, "and they don't need to make rules for every possible situation."[25]

Ms. Nearing is right. We hardly want to have companies codifying every possible behavior within the workplace so that it becomes ridiculously invasive. As discussed in Chapter 6, companies are already getting embroiled into worker's love lives by insisting on them signing "love contracts," which basically hold the employees to be acting of their own accord and rid the employer of any liability should the relationship derail. What's next? Employee donor cards kept in the human resources department that indicate who's willing to give up a kidney here or platelet cells there? That's not what I'm advocating. To grapple with complex issues and decisions in the workplace, what's called for is a frank discussion about the implications of the actions involved.

Not all readers of Ms. Nearing's and Mr. Helms' story failed to get this point. "I wholeheartedly agree that the company should have discussed the issues with both parties beforehand," wrote Jon K. Rust, a Harvard Business School student. "That being said, however, I wouldn't diminish in any way this subordinate's incredible generosity."[26]

That level of generosity is unquestioned. What drew so much attention to it was not only the transplant, but the unusual nature of the gesture. We're just not prepared to see such altruistic acts these days. Ms. Parks and her coauthors acknowledge this when they write:

In our individualistic culture, behavior which serves the welfare of others—whether episodic or routine—is typically described by theorists of human nature as "altruistic." But as the ethicist Alasdair MacIntyre has observed, the notion of "altruism" developed only in the eighteenth century in the wake of the ascent and triumph of the "ego-centric self." Since "human nature" was declared to be, at bottom, selfish, altruism became at once both necessary and impossible. Thus, "altruistic" behavior came to be seen as exceptional or even aberrant behavior.[27]

After the transplant operation, Ms. Nearing did sense that something was different in her relationship with Mr. Helms. For one thing, they and their families had become closer. Plus, she says, "I'm not 100 percent sure Art would ever fire me if he had to." If she felt she was getting favors she didn't deserve, she adds, "then I'd have to go find another job—and I don't want to."

Mr. Helms does say that he would be able to move Ms. Nearing to another job if, for example, she ever had a really tough year. "That's my job," he said. "I hire and I fire." But, he adds, "I had to make it clear to Nancy how much I appreciated what she did."

Most people compartmentalize their work lives from their personal lives. But as we spend more and more time in the workplace and our work seeps into our personal lives, the boundary between personal and business lives gets murkier. It's become harder to recognize that the personal decisions we make can have a huge impact on our lives at work and on those of the people who work with us.

We don't think twice of discussing the implications of our decisions with our family when they are directly affected. We ignore, however, discussing these same decisions with our coworkers when they are the ones directly involved. Robert N. Bellah, Richard Madsen, William M. Sullivan, Ann Swidler, and Steven M. Tipton observed in *Habits of the Heart: Individualism and Commitment in American Life* that the "manager's view of things is akin to that of the technician of industrial society par excellence, the engineer, except that the managers must admit interpersonal responses and personalities, including his own, into the calculation of effectiveness."[28] Those interpersonal responses might have included exploring how an unusual act between a worker and her boss would affect the overall workplace.

"If they don't discuss it in the workplace then they've got an elephant in the room," Ms. Parks says. "There's no way of predicting what the outcome may be."[29]

That, at some level, is what makes ethical decision making so formidable on a daily basis. The lines between our personal lives and our work lives seem to grow blurrier and blurrier. When issues do arise— as they seem to do more and more frequently these days—we just don't talk about them in the workplace unless a crisis arises. The challenge facing owners, managers, and employees is to figure out a way not to wait for the crisis to examine the implications of our acts and our decisions, but instead to recognize that ethical decisions may also include discussing actions from those such as sending routine e-mail that may seem benign to those truly noble acts of behavior of which no one dares or even thinks to explore the implications. It's only when we talk about the affects of the blurring lines that we can hope to find ways to make intelligent decisions about how to interpret, respond, and behave.

PART THREE

THE
COMMON
GOOD

*We cannot be the caring people whom our children need
us to be and ignore the world they will live in. We
cannot hide from the fact that without effective
democratic intervention and institution-building the
world economy might accelerate in ways that will tear our
lives apart and destroy the environment. Moral discourse
is essential in the family; it is also essential in the
world. There is no place to hide. "Distracted from
distraction by distraction" is how T.S. Eliot
characterized our situation. It is time to pay attention.*

—from *The Good Society* by Robert N. Bellah,
Richard Madsen, William M. Sullivan,
Ann Swidler, and Steven M. Tipton

By now it should be getting clearer how challenging it is to address the needs of the various constituencies facing you in your work life. Money decisions can affect the people you work with and the decisions you make about people can have immense financial implications. It also should be clear that more often than not it's difficult to unravel where the money decision stops and the people decision begins. That's not a bad thing.

The challenge, remember, is to elevate your awareness about the impact of your decisions on all the constituencies you affect and to try to make choices that address the needs of each as best you can. When it comes to dilemmas, no matter how much work you do, you still might come up short in addressing all the needs in play. But knowing that as you go ahead with your decisions is an important part of the ethical decision-making process. It not only makes you a more thoughtful, concerned businessperson, it also prepares you for where the potential brush-fires may flare up as a result of the choices you make.

The chapters in Part Three focus on how the decisions you make have an effect on the common good—the larger community in which you're doing business. The actions you take in business clearly have an impact on the world in which you're operating. So as part of your decision-making process, it's necessary to assess the needs of this constituency as well.

You'll see how businesspeople have grappled with dilemmas ranging from drawing the line between lying and posturing when doing business, how borrowing from competitors can, but shouldn't, lead to outright theft of ideas, and how difficult it is to align your personal beliefs with your business practices when facing an issue as challenging as minimizing the detrimental effect that what your company produces has on the environment.

After reading these chapters, you should begin to see even more clearly how the choices you make in business, particularly when facing thorny dilemmas, have an effect on money, people, and the common good. But more importantly, you'll gain an understanding that it's only after taking each of these constituencies into account that you can begin to get a full understanding of your business' potential to do good business.

8

True Lies

*L*ying has consequences.

That's an observation I made in an article once on how the actions of leaders can have a dramatic effect on how their followers will behave. But the consequences of lying go far deeper than just the worry that people will emulate you.

Our whole economic system works in large part because it's built on trust among the individuals involved. That trust—that I will do what you pay me to do and I will pay you for the services you do for me or the products you sell me—is fundamental to smooth dealings in the economy. This chapter looks at some of the consequences of lying as well as how people draw the line between lying and posturing for business advantage.

When there is a hint of fraud or untrustworthiness, a business runs the risk of losing customers who will cross the street to take their business elsewhere. When amazon.com, the behemoth purveyor of online books was accused of running advertisements disguised as editorials about titles on its site, it responded by making the distinction clearer. When it introduced its own online auction services to compete with the wildly successful eBay.com online auction, amazon.com capitalized on the news that the credibility of some of the merchandise that had been sold on eBay was being questioned by introducing a guarantee of up to $250 if buyers of goods on amazon.com's auctions were victims of fraud.

Sure, it was good advertising for amazon.com to take such an action. And certainly, it did prey on the unfortunate claims against one of its major online auction competitors. But it's a clear example that companies understand the importance of creating an image and a message that consumers can trust.

When I sat with her on a panel to discuss business ethics, Susan Spagnola, an attorney with Chase, summed up the consequences of lying nicely when she remembered a piece of wisdom her mother handed down to her: "Telling the truth takes a second; telling a lie takes a lifetime to undo."[1]

That simple piece of wisdom is echoed by Sissela Bok early in her book, *Lying: Moral Choice in Public and Private Life,* when she observes that "trust in some degree of veracity functions as a *foundation* of relations among human beings; when this trust shatters or wears away, institutions collapse."[2]

That need to trust in the veracity of others goes deep. But so, too, does the recognition that it's not something that necessarily comes easily. To get Biblical on you for a moment, consider the observations of theologian Max Stackhouse as he was trying to make clear that the 10 commandments of the Bible are just as relevant today as they were when they were written thousands of years ago. When it came time to talk about the ninth commandment, "You shall not bear false witness," Stackhouse reflected:

Lying, cheating, twisting information and evidence, creating false impressions, making what is bad look good, keeping silent when truth needs a voice, and failing to be direct are among the ways that we attempt to gain advantage or smooth human relations for our benefit. Though bargaining, sharp dealing, advertising, public relations, packaging, and selling 'as is' have been a part of economic life since the first horse trade, misrepresentation, deception, and obscurity by legalese infect open interaction and destroy the trust necessary for commerce. They lead to litigation in all things and even to the corruption of judicial systems. We are to tell the truth in all things, so far as we can know it.[3]

ROUTINE LIES CREATE ROUTINE EXPECTATIONS

In the column I wrote in *The New York Times* about lying having consequences, I went on to say that those consequences were "dire ones."[4] At the time, President Bill Clinton was in the midst of his impeachment hearings and Bill Gates was taking the stand in the antitrust trial in which Microsoft was embroiled. In an unfortunate turn of events, both Bills were caught giving sworn testimony that was less than truthful. President Clinton had just decided to bomb Iraq and some people were suggesting his actions were meant to deflect attention from his impeachment problem.

Clinton's credibility had been shattered and, as a result, he was finding his moves and motives on all issues called into question. At the same time all this was occurring, Bill Gates was appearing to dance around the truth under oath in the Microsoft antitrust trial and his credibility was also being called into question.

But just at the time that both Bills were caught up with truth troubles, they continued to be wildly popular. Both were among the top 10 most-admired men in America according to a Gallup poll that measures such things. It also came at a time when *Who's Who Among American High School Students* reported that 80 percent of high school students had admitted to cheating on school work according to its recent survey (95 percent said they were never caught).[5] In the light of such reports, it would seem that a little looseness with the truth shouldn't matter. But when you hear that at the same time businesses were reporting that they were losing somewhere between $40 billion and $250 billion annually due to employee theft,[6] you have to wonder if there isn't a strong connection. Follow the leader is an easy game to play in politics and business. Such behavior can ultimately cost a company dearly.

The thing is, lying should matter regardless of the bottom-line impact. For one, who wants to live in a nation of cheats and liars, never knowing if the person you're dealing with is being square? And here you have two prominent leaders—one from politics and one from business—seeming to suggest that lying was just a normal course of things you do to navigate your way through a difficult day. Such behavior doesn't just affect those two men; it can wreak havoc on the people who have put their trust in the leadership of these two. When lying seems to have taken hold at the top of an organization, the prospect for behavior in the rest of the organization is dim. It creates an atmosphere where the chief executive is sending down the message of "do as I say, not as I do."

"As long as there's this raging ambiguity and there's no accountability, people will start generating more and more lax responses to morally ambiguous situations," says Steven Berglas, a management consultant and a clinical psychologist at the Harvard Medical School. "Most people will start lowering standards for what's tolerable. And that manifests itself in people going along with what's being reinforced. People are going to lie for expediency."

I'm not suggesting that everybody should be able to tell every bit of truth every waking minute of every day. No one can manage that. We're faced daily with the task of trying to succeed by making choices about when to be vague or when something is better left unsaid.

Joseph L. Badaracco, a professor of business ethics at Harvard Business School and the author of *Defining Moments: When Managers*

Must Choose Between Right and Right, has said that "Not telling the full truth is different from outright lying. If you're going to run a big company or run the country, you can't put all your cards on the table; that's simply naive. Life is a series of different games, and you sort of play by the rules" when it comes to levels of candor in different circumstances.[7]

When you're negotiating in business, for example, clearly it's myopic to tip off at the outset what you're really after in a final deal. But even business school students appear to know the difference between posturing in a negotiation and outright lying. In a recent survey conducted by Professors Roy Lewicki of Ohio State's Fisher College of Business and Robert Robinson of the Harvard Business School among MBA students at Ohio State and Harvard, MBA students were asked to give a rating from 1 on the low end to 7 on the high end of the ethical proprietary of a variety of negotiating tactics. While they gave a high appropriateness rating (5.84) to "making an opening demand that is far greater than what one really hopes to settle for," they gave a much lower score (1.99) to "intentionally misrepresenting factual information to your opponent in order to support your negotiating arguments or position."[8]

We can make reasoned, responsible choices about how much of the truth we disclose during business dealings. Sissela Bok wrote that if "lies and truthful statements appear to achieve the same result or appear to be as desirable to the person contemplating lying the lies should be ruled out."[9]

It's not just during business negotiations that disclosing the entire truth may seem inappropriate. At times it can even seem barbaric to disclose the whole truth, as in the case where a doctor can choose how detailed to get when telling a dying patient how his health and body will deteriorate. Bok herself has observed: "There's great room for discretion, for knowing when not to speak."[10]

When Gates and Clinton took the courtroom stand, it wasn't a case of showing discretion. Instead—perhaps on the advice of their respective attorneys—Gates expressed that he wasn't sure of the meaning of a word as simple as "concerned" and Clinton wanted his questioner to clarify what was meant by the word "is."

Such self-defensive lies can ultimately inform everything you do. As a result, argues Bok, life turns into living a lie.[11] And when that happens to a leader, he or she can be sure that it will affect those who follow him.

There are indeed strong business reasons not to lie—none of these reasons will come as a huge surprise to anyone who has spent any time observing human behavior. "From a managerial point of view, you should have a strong prejudice toward being clear, direct and honest," says Joe Badaracco, because lying "becomes a bad habit. You might get caught. You set a bad example. The people who work with you probably aren't dumb; they'll copy what you do."[12]

So the real question for leaders like Bill Clinton or Bill Gates is that when their behavior becomes public, can they expect the people who work for them to aspire to any better behavior?

WHEN LIES DEFINE YOU

But a bigger challenge for people doing business today is to guard against becoming a person who begins to live a lie, how they can keep self-defensive lies permeating all they do. While some moralists may claim how simple it is to tell the truth all the time and that the truth will set you free, the reality is that it's not always so simple.

Psychologist Brad Blanton, author of the book *Radical Honesty,* for example, may argue that telling the truth is the only way for us to get beyond our adolescence and that "it hurts one not to tell the truth"[13] and that the mild stress disorders we suffer from are the direct result of the fact that we're all "trapped in lies," the truth is that it's just not that simple for most people to be totally honest all the time in their business dealings.

There are different degrees of wrongness to the variety of lies that can be told. Robert Solomon who writes about and teaches business ethics, observes, "Lying may always be wrong, but some lies are much more wrong than others. Truth may always be desirable, but the whole truth and nothing but the truth is just as likely to be a nightmare."[14]

A clear example of how businesspeople sometimes find themselves being less than totally truthful is when they're just starting their companies and they're trying to bootstrap—operate with little cash and generate growth from sales of products or services—their way up. Though it's rarely talked about, if you ask CEOs who started their companies with little cash, many of them will readily admit to an embellishment here and a fabrication there.

Every year, *Inc.* magazine publishes a list of the 500 fastest-growing private companies in the United States. One year, the magazine surveyed the CEOs of companies on the 1995 and 1996 Inc. 500 lists who said they had grown their businesses with little or no capital. Of those who responded, 14 percent said that bootstrapping, by definition, requires "unsavory business practices." I was curious about what kind of behavior they would lump into the "unsavory" category, so I called them to find out. For some entrepreneurs, "unsavory" involved stringing out a supplier on a payment or two, but for others it meant out-and-out lying.[15]

"Sometimes when you're backed up against the wall, your instincts take over, and you do what you have to do to survive," says Nick Molina, remembering the early days of his company, Let's Talk Cellular & Wireless, which sells cellular phones.[16]

When you're first starting a business, all you can really do is sell people on your idea for what you and your fledgling company can do. After all, customers, vendors, employees, and all of the other businesspeople you come in contact with want some reassurance that they're involved with a CEO of substance, someone who exudes confidence and gives off a sense of stability, who exudes success.

"When you're small and you're trying to establish larger contracts, obviously you'll attempt to do everything you can to make customers believe you're of size and capable of doing the work," says Neal DeAngelo, cofounder of DeAngelo Brothers, a landscape-management company in Hazleton, Pennsylvania. But DeAngelo argues that "it's just not true" that "people who go into business with no money have to lie."

DeAngelo may be right, but for some in business, they find that it sure comes in handy. When, for example, Molina's company was peddling cellular phones and pagers out of a van, he admits that falling short of the truth was practically a standard practice. Consider what he had to do to get Let's Talk Cellular space in the Dadeland Mall, in Miami. He was having trouble getting the leasing agent for the mall to take his calls and, more important, to take him seriously. "I called every day and could never get past the secretary," says Molina. "Then one day I called up and she asked me who was calling. I said, 'Tell him this is his doctor and it's a family emergency.' " The leasing agent took the call, and Molina got the time to charm him.

But that's not the end of the story. When the leasing agent told Molina that to be considered, companies needed to be "established," Molina took that to mean he needed to have been in business for at least two years. "So we manipulated our financials, and we lied our way through that and said, 'Yes, we have,' " reports Molina, who says he had actually been in business for six months. When the leasing agent told him that his central place of business had to occupy a "substantial" amount of square footage to be considered, Molina says, "We put a wide-angle camera in a corner and filled up the office with friends, family, and employees, and just took pictures so it looked like a very busy office." Then, according to Molina, they told the leasing agent that their central office contained more square footage than it actually did. For good measure, "We parked our van in front of a building and took a picture of it and made it sound like that was our building," says Molina.

Molina's story suggests that a stockpile of untruths can be as handy as a reservoir of cash. That just isn't true. Oh sure, there's a lot of posturing that goes on when companies get started, but there's a qualitative difference between lying and posturing. It's one thing to send a photo of a busy workplace to a leasing agent hoping that he'll assume it's larger than it is. It's quite another to tell him that you have more square footage than you do. Most companies have postured at some point in their history to win a client or grow the company. But posturing is different from lying.

Many CEOs who read the story of the CEOs who said it took unsavory behavior to bootstrap a company clearly understand the difference. An owner of an employee benefits firm in Massachusetts wrote: "Posturing, embellishing, or 'selling the sizzle' are as old as business." But he continued, "On the other hand, manipulating financials, holding vendor money, bending agreements, and other less-than-honest actions are unacceptable. Those actions ultimately create less trust in the marketplace."[17]

THE DIFFERENCE BETWEEN POSTURING AND LYING

When you're just starting up a company, nobody expects you to come right out and blurt: "I don't yet have any track record, so I don't really know if I can do what I say I can do. Besides, I don't really have the employees in place to do the work anyway." Prospective partners of any kind—suppliers, employees, customers—judge you partly on your ability to convince them that you're going to be able to deliver on your grandiose plans. So you talk enthusiastically, you bid aggressively, you lease office space that's a tad nicer than what you can really afford. That's posturing. Lying is a different story.

Everybody postures. Consider the whole practice of bargaining. Stephen Carter, observes in his book *Integrity* that a "weakness in conceiving integrity as mere honesty and conceiving honesty as telling all that you know is that it would make bargaining impossible. When we bargain, by definition we take positions that are not our final positions. I see a house that is listed for sale at $100,000. I wish to buy it and decide that I will pay the asking price if necessary, but my first offer is just $75,000. The owner responds, 'I am sorry to say that I cannot take a dollar less than $95,000.' I answer: 'My absolute top is $80,000.' Now, I am not telling the truth, and neither, I suspect, is the owner of the house, but we are not really being dishonest either, and we certainly are not acting without integrity."[18]

The truth is that when we go to buy a house, a car, or any number of things for which bargaining is expected, when we make our first offer, we're low-balling—if we're smart. And so is the person who comes back to us with his first price. We're both posturing to try to get the deal that works. Are we being ruthlessly honest about every detail of what our personal finances will let us afford? No, but then that would be just plain dumb in the context of buying a house or a car.

Anybody who manages a company knows that there are times when saying nothing—and, as a result, letting employees' imaginations run wild with their assumptions—is far wiser than disclosing everything. "The one time I decided to just be honest with our employees about our company's precarious financial condition," recalls an Inc. 500 CEO I'd interviewed as part of the "unsavory tactics" canvassing, "I called all of my people together and said: 'Look, we're handing out payroll checks, but we're broke. If you have to cash your check, I understand. But this is where we are financially. Could you guys just hold off cashing your checks for a week?' All 40 employees ran to the bank that day." The CEO, who requested anonymity, says that if the situation were to happen again, he certainly wouldn't be as truthful.

Most people understand that in certain situations posturing is not only appropriate, it's expected. It's often even appreciated.

When, for example, Magic Box, a provider of local- and wide-area computer networks, had its first brochures designed, it featured multiple departments and capabilities for the company. The thing was that the brochure actually listed more departments than the company had employees. "We would look like we were a multidepartment company when we were only three or four people at the time," says co-founder Israel Fintz. "We departmentalized everything, and basically, I was doing all of it. But I never lied and said we had seven people when we had just four." Fintz was giving prospective customers wide latitude in assuming what his company was capable of doing. He wasn't misinforming them.

What Posturing Looks Like

Posturing takes form in what seems like a countless number of variations. In canvassing the CEOs of former *Inc.* 500 companies about various posturing tactics they used when growing their companies, several classic examples surfaced, including:

- *Customers can't live without us.* When Jim Zona, CEO of Pittsburgh Plastics, was trying to sell his company's shoe-insole inserts to retail outlets, he'd have someone stop in a store and ask if it carried Gel-Soles. Two days later, he'd have somebody else stop at the same store. After a few days, he'd have a salesperson call on the store to see if it wanted to carry his product. "And they'd say, 'Come on down,' " recalls Zona. "Once we got in those stores, we'd tell everybody to go there to buy the product."

- *Sure, we can do that.* To get started and bring in much-needed capital, Steve Burkhart, cofounder of Advanced Micro-Electronics, a Vincennes, Indiana, computer-maintenance company, put a bid on the service contract for a local university. The problem was that he didn't have a clue how to price the contract or what would be involved in maintaining all the computers on campus. "We just didn't know a lot of things at that point," says Burkhart. He bid $41,000 with payment due up front. Since everyone else bid more than $100,000, Advanced Micro got the job. The college never asked for references. The college remained a customer, and Burkhart says he kept bidding on projects he knew nothing about. "Right now we're trying to put together a bid for seven GE plants in Mexico. We don't have a clue how to do international business," he says.

- *I've got a closet full of people.* In 1990, when Robert Luster started Luster Construction Management, a San Francisco-based consulting firm that caters to large construction projects, he couldn't afford to hire any employees. "But," he says, "I had 25 individuals I'd already interviewed that as I found a job I could hire." That's how Luster says he built his business. He had permission from the 25 applicants to use their resumes, which he would bring to prospective construction-project clients. "In professional services," says Luster, "they're not so much interested in the company as in the individual you can deliver."

The posturing that all of these company CEOs undertook (and there are countless more examples that any business owner can add to the list) was done with the sole aim of painting a picture of a company that was more established than it was. When Luster promised to deliver "his" employees to the site, he simply did what every good company owner tries to do when starting out on a shoestring—exude confidence, determination, and ruthless optimism. Certainly, that's often done with the goal of trying to get the upper hand in a business relationship.

But—and this is a big "but" here: You have to be clear, and make clear to the people with whom you are doing business, that you are not going to do just anything to get that upper hand. You have to make clear and be clear in your own mind that you will not cross the line and start lying to your customers. Because once you cross that line, it's difficult to stem the tide of your own lies. It takes a rigorous commitment to keep foremost in your mind the difference between putting on a good face and blatantly lying about your credentials, your business, your services, or your products.

CROSSING THE LINE

In the introduction to her book *Lying*, Sissela Bok stressed that her "main task will not be to produce a sordid catalogue of falsehoods and corrupt dealings, nor to go over once again what each day's newspaper reveals about deception in high places. Rather, I want to stress the more vexing dilemmas of ordinary life; dilemmas which beset those who think that their lies are too insignificant to matter much, and others who believe that lying can protect someone or benefit society. We need to look most searchingly, not at what we would all reject as unconscionable, but at those cases where many see *good reasons* to lie."[19] When you're just starting a business and are strapped for cash it's all too easy to justify why it's necessary for you to blur that line—in fact, cross that line from posturing into outright lying to stay in business.

Once you cross that line, however, it's an easy slide to where you, like Molina of Let's Talk Cellular & Wireless, start referring to your most questionable strategies as "actually pretty innovative" rather than recognizing them for what they are. Molina says he developed his "innovative" strategy when his vendors grew tired of late payments from him and required cash on delivery. His technique involved using a check embosser to imprint amounts on a blank check, and typing "certified check" on it so the delivery person would leave the inventory for which he was supposed to get cash or a certified check. That would give Molina a couple of days to actually get some money in the bank. "When the vendor got their check, they'd call and say, 'Hey, this is a regular check,' and we'd say, 'Oh, I'm sorry. Just send it back and we'll send you a cashier's check.' And then they'd say, 'Oh no, we'll just cash this one.' "

What's wrong with such lying anyway? Well, we'd like to believe folks like DeAngelo, the cofounder of the landscape-management company, who argues that "once you get a reputation for being a cheat, a liar, a stealer, you're not going to last very long in any industry."

DeAngelo's advice is well-taken and shared by many, including Stephen Carter who observed in his book *Integrity* that "in all but the most extreme cases, leaders will do well to recognize that the judgment on whether they possess integrity will be based in part on whether they are willing to be forthright in the face of risk—not on how skilled they are in the arts of deception and evasion."[20]

Sadly, depending on how you define "long," predictions such as DeAngelo's don't always seem to be the case. Everyone has heard stories of company owners who have lied and stayed in business nonetheless.

One problem with this is that when you're convinced your survival depends on a lie, short-term thinking takes hold and you can lose sight of the fact that long-term you may have lost your credibility in the marketplace.

Another problem, too, is that, like the cases of Bill Clinton and Bill Gates, if you're the leader of a company and you blur the rules, the folks in your company don't know what's acceptable behavior anymore. In fact, employees may decide that it's not only okay to lie as the boss does, but that it's the only way to get ahead in this company. When employees mirror such behavior, the consequences can get ugly. "Beginning early on to stretch the truth or to lie outright sets a dangerous precedent and gives license to other employees around you," says a vice president of an insurance company based in Georgia.[21] Employees who sense a culture where lying is acceptable may think that that goes for stealing as well.

Sadly, lying is often the result of laziness or habit more than anything else. It's "only where a lie is a *last resort* can one even begin to consider whether or not it is morally justified," observes Bok. "Mild as this initial stipulation sounds, it would, if taken seriously, eliminate a great many lies told out of carelessness or habit or unexamined good intentions."[22]

That's a very good rule of thumb: Don't even consider lying unless you've explored every other option and it is indeed the last resort. And even then you need to wrestle with the question of whether the lie you are about to tell has any moral justification. So here's some practical, bottom-line business advice: Don't lie. Just don't do it.

While there are many concerns about the effect of lying in business, the biggest concern about lying becoming acceptable behavior was articulated by that CEO who had requested anonymity in the "unsavory activity" canvassing. He asked me: "Aren't you concerned that some people will take some of these ideas and say, 'Hey, why didn't I think of that?' "

Ultimately, that is the price you pay for allowing lies to become an acceptable way of doing business. Once you're recognized for what you are, then your employees, your customers, and your vendors will think nothing of turning around and lying to you to get what they need. The real fear is that the lies we tell will come back to be the lies we're told. And worse yet, that as another admired leader is caught in a sworn lie, we become a nation of liars where no one knows the rules of the game.

If trust in your partners in commerce erodes enough, the time you could be spending doing your job or running your business gives way to trying to figure out whether someone's lying to you. The game becomes to catch someone in a lie before you're caught lying yourself. You're forced to lie, you tell yourself, because it's expected and that you're naïve if you don't.

The business of business should be to make or create something the public wants to buy. When it becomes a game of lies, it's easy to lose sight of that. That's not why you got into business and it's not how you want to do business—or have business done to you. Long-term—and it's tough to have a long-term mentality in a short-term world—you can't sustain a business built on lies. Long-term you lose the customer's faith, the employee's loyalty, and possibly you're own job or position. Besides being wrong, lying just isn't worth the risk.

9

❀

Spies Like Us

O ne of the byproducts of covering the workplace and business ethics beat is that readers tend to get confessional on me. After a story runs, I get calls or e-mail messages from readers who have either been the victim or the victimizer in some particularly harrowing ordeal that might or might not relate to whatever topic I'd thought I'd written about or that I thought I'd get response to.

Mostly the confessors are victims and are seeking some sort of redress for their suffering, which, of course, I'm in no position to give them. In fact, as I tell them, I'm not really in any position to advise them on what they should do since I rarely get both sides of the story. But they continue to call and I try my best to point them in some useful direction.

Those are the victims. And while their stories are interesting, the more intriguing responses come from the victimizers. It's as if they've bottled up their guilt for years over some action or series of transgressions that they know was wrong and now seize the opportunity to get matters off their chest. More frequently than not, they make clear that their particular stories are not for attribution, but that they think I should cover an event similar to one like theirs because for them that event had a huge impact on how they run their business.

One company owner in particular calls me regularly to tell me what topics he thinks I should cover and then he proceeds to fill me in on his own experiences, most often as the guy who crosses the line of ethical behavior. On one such occasion, I returned home late one evening and when I retrieved my voicemail messages on my home office phone, there was a message from this company owner commenting on a story of mine he'd just read (in which he'd been quoted anonymously), but going on to tell me that he thought I should tackle the subject of corporate espionage because, to hear him tell it, it was huge.

It was late in the evening, but since he lives on the West Coast and I on the East, I gave him a call to find out if something in particular had happened that caused him to suggest that corporate espionage was such a huge issue. At first he talked a bit about how his competitors were always trying to get into his plant to find out his procedures so they might be able to undercut his prices. But as we kept talking, it became clear that what was really eating at my CEO friend was the fact that he had spent a good deal of time in the early years of his company spying on his own suppliers and competitors. So he knew how easy it was.

He told me how he used to drive his company truck to one supplier in particular for pickups. This supplier was able to manufacture a part he needed for the product he sold that his company hadn't been able to figure out how to make yet. He grew tired of having to pay a premium for this particular part and thought it would be much more efficient for them to make it themselves. So to find out how they tooled the machinery to make the part, he posed as a truck driver to pick up the goods. Early one morning when he went to make the pickup, he parked his truck, and then in a seemingly innocent manner, walked inside the company to use the men's room which was only accessible if you cut across the shop floor where all the tooling machinery was. The confessional CEO told me how he made at least a half-dozen trips in and out of that company that one morning, each time drawing sketches on small pieces of paper that reflected what he saw on the competitor's shop floor. No one caught on and within weeks, his own company had developed the tooling necessary to make the part that this competitor had formerly supplied.

As with every conversation I'd had with this guy, it ended with my telling him that his was a fascinating story and that I really think readers would get a lot from hearing him tell how vulnerable they are to corporate espionage. He hemmed and hawed, finishing the conversation with some reflection along these lines: "Well geez, I don't really know if I want other people to know this stuff. What's to keep them from copying it and doing it themselves?"

Well, yeah, that's a problem. And it's an indication of just how wrong this CEO knew his behavior to be. He'd trespassed and stolen information from a competitor. He certainly wouldn't want a competitor of his to victimize him in the same manner. Who would?

SOMEONE IS AFTER YOUR INFORMATION

But here's the rub. When you're in a highly competitive market, it makes sense that you want to get as much information as you can about what your competitors are doing so that you have a better understanding of what you're up against, what market opportunities exist, and how others are tackling similar challenges. At the same time, you probably have your own proprietary information that you want to protect from getting into your competitors' hands. And if you believe the press reports, it seems inevitable that someone's after your information.

In the spring of 1999, *Time* magazine ran a story in its business section titled, "Eyeing the Competition," with the subtitle: "Corporate espionage is so pernicious that the U.S. passed a law to curb it. But

in today's global economy, dirty tricks are all in a day's work." As if
to make matters more ominous, the author, Daniel Eisenberg, pointed
out that since the Economic Espionage Act of 1996 was signed by President Clinton, "only 13 criminal cases have gone to indictment."[1]

Yet, stories of companies finding themselves embroiled in corporate spying abound. And, when caught, the end result can be costly.

In May 1999, Lexington, Massachusetts-based Raytheon Aerospace
Company settled a lawsuit that alleged it had used the services of a security firm to spy on AGES, one of its competitors, in its Alabama factory. Raytheon allegedly had used the services of the security firm to
perform audio and video surveillance over a three-day period, as well
as to take documents from the competitor. Just days before the case
went to trial, Raytheon, without admitting wrongdoing, settled the
case for $16 million.[2]

There are also times when companies engage in corporate espionage
to right an apparent wrongdoing. Back in 1989, before he could decide
whether to take legal action against FiberView, a competitor who was
allegedly stealing trade secrets from him, Steven R. Sedlmayr, the CEO
of ADTI, a fiber-optics company in Colorado, drove to the competitor's company site late one night to see for himself. When he got there,
he shined a flashlight into FiberView's offices.

"My jaw dropped," he told Ed Welles, a colleague of mine at *Inc.*
magazine. "I could have been looking at the back of our shop."[3]

What Sedlmayr saw were parts that he recognized as proprietary
to his company. He then went over to the garbage dumpster, climbed
in, and found drawings of parts that his company manufactured as well
as a payroll which listed former employees of his. In all, he gathered
four bags of garbage. After he sorted through the material, he called
his lawyer.

"My adrenaline was running at that point," he said. "I was really
mad. I couldn't believe that anyone would be so stupid as to copy exactly what we do."

The evidence was enough for U.S. Marshals to go to FiberView's
offices and impound the premises. There they found more material
that suggested theft from ADTI.

Ultimately, the judge in the case found in favor of Sedlmayr, issuing biting comments about Brett Kingstone, FiberView's founder: "I find Mr. Kingstone to be 100 percent incredible. I don't believe a thing he says," wrote Judge Lewis T. Babcock of the U.S. District Court in Colorado. "I find as a matter of fact, Mr. Kingstone set out to and did, in fact, misappropriate ADTI's entire process . . . [FiberView] literally picked up the process, lock, stock, and barrel, and took it from ADTI's shop and put it in FiberView's shop."

Steven Sedlmayr had engaged in a little spying himself to counteract the theft of trade secrets of which his company had been the victim. And that gets at one of the chief ethical conundrums you face when you deal with issues of how far to go when gathering intelligence on a competitor. Just like the CEO who calls me regularly to tell me of how he's worried about someone spying on him, you have to ask yourself if it's any surprise that you're being spied on if you're doing some less-than-savory spying yourself.

How Real Is the Corporate Espionage Threat?

How much danger is there that your company may fall prey to the same type of infiltration from the competitive enemy? Well, it depends on who you ask. Some estimates suggest that as much as $100 billion is lost every year because of espionage.[4] Other estimates, while more conservative are no less daunting. In a survey done by Richard J. Heffernan, a Branford, Connecticut consultant, for the American Society for Industrial Security, the 172 companies that responded said they had on an annual basis $31 billion dollars "at risk in actual, attempted, and suspected cases of trade secret theft." Of course, those numbers depend on how the companies reporting define "suspected" cases.

Some believe that the numbers belie the frequency of the problem. "Is it going on regularly?" asks Patrick J. Gnazzo, vice president of business practices and chief ethics officer at United Technologies

Corp., a $24.7 billion corporation that owns Carrier, Otis Elevator, Pratt & Whitney, Sikorksy Helicopter, among others. "I don't think so. Is it a big problem? Of course it is."[6]

There does indeed seem to be a growing concern about just how vulnerable proprietary company information is. From the number of books published on the subject alone, you'd think that corporate espionage was the top concern on every businessperson's mind. When the books are published, most are done so in the guise of advising readers how to protect themselves against being the victim of corporate espionage. But it takes little extrapolation to know that what the reader is also getting is advise on how to do a little snooping of his own.

In his book *Corporate Espionage: What It Is, Why It's Happening in Your Company,* Ira Winkler comments on how easy it is for sales and marketing employees to fall prey to spies seeking your company's information: "Take your sales-and-marketing department," he writes. "Its job is to get the word out about your products or services. In this highly competitive marketplace, salespeople often leak information about upcoming offerings to potential customers. They give up key details, scheduling information, and product specifications, all in the service of making the sale. They don't do it to cause problems. For the most part, it's a matter of honest enthusiasm."

Now that you know you can wheedle the information you want out of enthusiastic salespeople, Mr. Winkler continues: "Your sales-and-marketing people have a job to do, but you have to make sure they're not undermining your security efforts when they do it. At trade shows, anyone expressing a sincere interest in a marketer's products can get just about any information he or she could want. Salespeople are supposed to give out information, not protect it. On almost all occasions, if a sale is in jeopardy, sensitive information will be revealed. Trained corporate spies know how to pose as interested customers and how to drag out a purchase negotiation until they get the information they want."[7]

If you're shrewd and persistent enough, it is indeed possible to get information from your competitors that they'd probably rather you not have. You could make the argument that most folks in business would rather stick to their own business plan than to simply copy or base their decisions on what their competitors are doing. But then there is a lot that companies can learn from one another and many have done a good job of using other companies methods to benchmark their own way of doing business. When benchmarking is done, however, it's with the full knowledge of both parties involved.

Corporate espionage experts will tell you how vulnerable every company is to having their secrets stolen. And often, the way the information is gathered is decidedly low-tech. A crumpled napkin with writing on it, an overheard conversation between two employees sitting together on an airplane, a product specification sheet left on the sink in the men's room of a conference trade show hall are among the methods that almost all the published books will list as prime targets for secret stealing.

What most every corporate espionage expert will tell you as well is that the industry associations (such as the Society for Competitive Intelligence Professionals and the National Association of Legal Investigators) have written codes of ethics. But neither those codes nor a plethora of tips and tactics do much to help the businessperson who is trying to decide how far he wants to go in gathering information on a competitor.

Where to Draw the Line in Gathering Information

The dilemma facing most people in business when it comes to gathering information is how far you're willing to let yourself go. Do you ignore your competitors and risk having them overtake your market position either through sheer superiority of product or service, or from information they gathered on your company? Do you aggressively set out to gather as much information on your competitor as possible so you're not caught by surprise and can tailor your own business decisions to stay one step ahead of the next guy? In a very competitive market, the difficult decision you have to make is to know where to draw the line.

Okay, where do you start? Well, first off, you can put on the side of what's off limits anything that requires breaking the law to steal trade secrets and proprietary information from competitors. That these actions are wrong is a no-brainer. Bribing people, breaking into their offices, interviewing prospective employees from competitors as a ruse to get them to spill trade secrets are all maneuvers that cross the legal lines and it makes sense to avoid such practices.

In a discussion with Christopher E. Bogan, CEO of Best Practices, LLC in Chapel Hill, North Carolina, and coauthor of *Benchmarking for Best Practices: Winning Through Innovative Adaptation,* he might have been stating the obvious when he observed: "Eventually these things do come back to haunt. In business it's foolish to think that you can tell employees that they can play outside the boundaries once. They'll play outside the boundaries a second, third, and fourth time. If you get caught and you're a public company, your stock will take a hit. If you're a private company, your customers and vendors will wonder whether they can trust what you share with them."[8]

But that still leaves you with having to decide how far you'll go to get competitive information without breaking the law. The idea of borrowing good ideas from other companies just makes good business sense. And it's ridiculous to allow fear of litigation to keep you from making such sound business decisions as hiring good employees who may bring with them an expertise they learned at the feet of your competitor. Who doesn't want to hire good, experienced people?

There are plenty of clever ways to gain competitive intelligence without engaging in questionable behavior. You just have to decide which, if any, you're comfortable using. Tom Peters, the author of *In Search of Excellence,* for example, recalls one such tactic he used. "I remember when I was working with Xerox's copier division, they'd figured out when Kodak was getting ready for a new product launch by counting the cars in the parking lot at a particular building where

Kodak was known to do its training. Now that kind of stuff is fabulous and completely legit."[9]

But this still begs the question: Where do you draw the line? Well, the bottom line is that if the action you're taking—whether it's routing through someone's garbage or hiring a private investigator to check out the backgrounds of prospective employees you lose to the competition—is something that you'd be embarrassed to have your customers, suppliers, investors, employees, or other people you do business with find out, there's a good chance you've crossed the line. That old mirror test where Peter Drucker and others suggest thinking about whether you can look at yourself in the mirror every morning after you've done what you've done can come in handy.

"You have to have somebody who is looking beyond whether this is legal or not and addressing the question of does it feel right?" says UTC's Gnazzo. "Are we comfortable with it? Do we want to be perceived as being a company that operates in this particular manner?"[10]

The problem is that when you're in the moment, you lose sight of the bigger picture. The exhilaration of pulling out a competitor's customer list from its weekly trash bin can blind you to the fact that, "hey, we're going through trash here." And is going through someone's trash really why you got into business in the first place?

INCHING OVER THE LINE BY LOSING PERSPECTIVE

Losing perspective on why you're doing what you're doing can result in an inching over that line you swore you would never cross in business. Slowly, over time, the original intention of some program or effort can get lost and somehow you find yourself with a company culture that is thoroughly out of whack.

It can happen at the best of companies. D. Clark Ogle, the chief executive of Johnston Industries, a $300-million textile manufacturer based in Columbus, Georgia, knows this firsthand. His company, he says, has been the victim of corporate espionage. And the alleged culprit is Milliken & Company, the giant private textile manufacturer, which has 16,000 employees and in 1989 was the recipient of the Malcolm Baldrige Quality Award in manufacturing.

As it happens, Johnston isn't the only company to claim that Milliken & Company infiltrated its ranks. Milliken had already settled a lawsuit brought by NRB Industries, a New York-based textile firm, that claimed Milliken had hired a consultant who posed as an investor and another who posed as a graduate student to gain access to its corporate secrets. Johnston first suspected that they were victims of the same scam during the discovery process of NRB's trial.

Apparently, it didn't stop with Johnston Industries. In that same discovery process, it was alleged that over the period scanning 1994 to 1997, seven other companies were cited as also having been spied on for proprietary information. Each company was allegedly given its own code name by the Milliken operatives.[11]

Armed with the information from the NRB suit, Johnston Industries decided to sue Milliken. In turn Milliken released a statement that it would defend itself "vigorously" and cited one of its long-standing policies that forbade its employees or consultants from illegally obtaining proprietary information from competitors. Once "claims were made about the propriety of the collection techniques being used" by the consultants, the statement said, "Milliken ceased doing business with these consultants."[12]

Johnston's Ogle is convinced of the havoc that the corporate espionage wreaked on his company's bottom line. "Obviously, the things Milliken did hurt us," said Ogle. "They took away opportunities our people had found for niches we were exploiting somewhat on our own. Then, basically overnight, we had a competitor in there knowing our processes."[13]

How did Milliken, a winner of the esteemed Malcolm Baldrige Award and a company profiled for its excellent practices by writers ranging from Tom Peters and Nancy Austin in *Passion for Excellence:*

The Leadership Difference to Christopher Bogan in *Benchmarking for Best Practices: Winning Through Innovative Adaptation* end up in such a fix?

Perhaps part of the answer lies in one particular aspect of the company that irks Mr. Ogle. And that's that the company, he argues, takes pride in its corporate mantra to "steal ideas shamelessly." This notion of stealing ideas shamelessly is not something that is terribly original to Milliken. It's an idea that first started to be touted around widely in the late 1980s and is still a hallmark of companies that practice benchmarking. It was never meant as some rallying cry to encourage companies to steal their competitors' trade secrets or to break the law to get them.

"The concept of steal shamelessly is really grounded on the concept of don't be afraid to borrow," says benchmarking consultant Christopher Bogan. In the book he coauthored with Michael J. English, the authors cite Milliken's practice of quoting the corporate slogan "steal shamelessly."[14]

"It's a dramatic statement that says no individual, no company, no team, no industry can corner all good ideas," says Bogan. "It doesn't for a minute suppose that you should steal proprietary information or trade secrets without the permission of the originators of that content."

That might have been the original intention of Milliken's mantra, but Ogle believes that using the "stealing" to stand in for benchmarking practices sends the wrong message to the company's employees. "When you take something that has negative connotations, just the subliminal message you send to your culture is different," he says.

Is it possible that that subliminal message rather than what might have been its original intended meaning seeped into what was deemed acceptable behavior at the company. Tom Peters who's been following Milliken & Company for years and wrote extensively about the company in *Passion for Excellence: The Leadership Difference*,[15] was not totally surprised when he heard the allegations about Milliken's behavior.

"From my experience, the ethical standard there is very high," says Peters. "But they are also a very aggressive company. If you have an action-at-all-costs mentality, even if your ethical standards are high, sometimes people are pushed to do stuff they shouldn't have done."

One possible explanation for what went wrong is that while the original meaning of the aggressive, yet harmless phrase "steal shamelessly" might have been well-known to the employees and managers who were on board when it was first chanted as a rallying cry, that meaning may not be clear to the perhaps thousands of employees at Milliken who are relatively new to the world of business.

When the phrase first started to be used widely in the 1980s, it wasn't all that common for companies to acknowledge borrowing ideas from one another. There was a strong bias against anything "not invented here." Today, it's more common than ever to grab good ideas from competitors as well as to share your own. (In fact, one of the hallmarks of the Malcolm Baldrige Award which Milliken had won is to open up your company for others to tour.)

"The good news is that people love to share stuff," Tom Peters says of the fact that benchmarking and concepts like "stealing ideas shamelessly" have taken hold. But there's potentially some bad news here as well if the original intent of the message is not made clear to all employees and they misinterpret what it is that their beloved company wants them to do.

Chris Bogan, the benchmarking consultant, warns: "It's very easy to misinterpret what benchmarking is and what good it can provide for organizations, because people will wrongly think it condones illicit behavior."

"People at Johnston are highly motivated, but we're not ethically challenged," says Johnston Industries' Ogle. Well, the truth is, we're all ethically challenged. When it comes to issues like crossing the line to gain information on competitors, the question is: How do we step up to that challenge?

The real ethical challenge in the case like the one involving Milliken is for businesspeople to make sure that that misinterpretation doesn't happen. Again, here's a case that cries for good management skills. Rather than assume employees understand the subtleties of a rallying cry formed decades ago, managers need to do their job and make it clear that they want their employees to go out and aggressively do their jobs, while at the same time making it clear that it's equally important to not do anything that's untoward or illegal in the process.

The Milliken case begs the question: Can you, when you're an aggressive company, send the right message to employees? Peters thinks you can. "State your case very clearly: 'Yes, we are aggressive. Yes, we are action-oriented. But if there's anything that ever shows up gray on your record, ethically speaking, you're either in serious trouble or you're out of here.' "

One thing any good manager can do is to decide what he'd have to do if the actions about to be undertaken were ever found out. Would he have to fire the employee for doing it? In the press statement it released, Milliken says it took that very action.

The trouble with taking action after the events have occurred, however, is that it seems to send the message that it's okay to do whatever it is you did as long as you don't get caught. The message that some behavior won't be tolerated needs to be sent loud and clear to employees beforehand, with as much zeal as "steal shamelessly" had when it was first being touted around as a rally cry in the 1980s.

Mr. Peters only partly jokes that companies should consider amending the phrase to now read "steal shamelessly and ethically"[16] and paste that throughout the company. Or better yet, a good slogan for any manager in business would be: Play hard, but play clean.

10

Whole Earth Policy

Increasingly, the awareness of business' impact on the environment is coming into sharper focus. We read stories in the newspaper about barges full of waste that no one wants. We hear of communities fighting the creation of a toxic waste dump that must go somewhere, anywhere, as long as it's not in our neighborhood. As a result of hearing and seeing the stress we as people in the community and business are placing on the environment, we begin to notice things in the workplace that we might have overlooked in the past.

Even companies that produce no products on site begin to recognize that merely keeping operations going takes a toll on the environment. Take technology, for example. Wasn't it supposed to have given us the paperless office? Instead, we're awash in paper, moreso than ever before. Well, where does all that used paper go? And even if we have a recycling program at work, are we indeed creating more waste than we ever did before because technology (our computers, printers, and copiers) lets us print out version after version after version rather than the final or close to final drafts of our reports, memos, recipes from that Internet site, and list of jokes making the e-mail rounds?

We notice the empty toner cartridges for the copying machine piling up and, while we know there's something bad about tossing them in the trash rather than recycling them, we really don't know if we've be making much of a dent in the problem. Should we send the empty cartridges out to be refilled? Is that better? It seems trivial to worry about matters such as these, but it's gotten to the point where we can't even grab a cup of coffee from the communal coffee pot and make a clear decision about whether a paper cup (that needs to be thrown out and creates more paper waste) is better than a mug (all those soap suds getting into the water stream; all that excess water used) for the environment.

We notice the little things and then we start thinking about the bigger things our company may be doing that're harmful to the environment. Sometimes it's obvious if we're in businesses that make products that are widely known to be harmful. Other times we have an inkling that all that smoke pumping out of the manufacturing plant can't possibly be good for the environment. And then even those of us in apparently benign businesses such as magazine publishing begin to wonder if the ink being used on the paper—all that paper—is toxic when it hits the landfill and whether those soy-based inks we'd read about are really any good as alternatives.

The awareness may hit us on a personal level in what we do or on a corporate level in what our company does, but it will hit us at some point. And while many employees and managers may give up when faced with the complexity of the problem and the often conflicting solutions, that awareness only builds.

When that awareness grows more acute, Paul Hawken, one of the more articulate writers on business and the environment wonders "how long a company can prevail if its employees, consciously or unconsciously, perceive their products, processes, or corporate goals as harmful to humankind."[1]

Environmental thinkers and writers like Hawken, John Elkington of Sustainability, an environmental consulting company in London, Tim Weiskel, director of the Harvard Seminar on Environmental Values, and many others are doing the difficult work of sorting out how we can continue to work and live a productive life without doing harm to the environment. But what I'd like to look at in this chapter are some stories that try to get at how people in business think about these complex issues that require them to go through the process of making ethical decisions.

Throughout the process of researching and writing this book, what has fascinated me is how people think about ethical decision making. That's true of the stories in this chapter as well. There are two primary stories here and they cover the topic of response to the environmental issues from two very different sides. One has to do with how a company that is found to be doing harm (and breaking the law) responds to getting caught, why they might be responding as they do, and how people in the community react. The other story has to do with a CEO who is in a business that contradicts his strong beliefs as the self-avowed environmentalist he is in his personal life, and what he decides to do about the conflict.

The stories taken together illustrate a simple point: Even when we strongly believe in something, we often allow ourselves to justify behaving in a way that goes against all that we believe. When we do that, we run the risk of losing credibility in the community as well as creating a discomfort within ourselves. The question for you in your business is whether you can be productive in a setting that increasingly causes you such discomfort.

DOING THE RIGHT THING WHEN YOU'RE CAUGHT DOING WRONG

In an exchange I was having with Jon Gunnemann, a social ethicist who teaches at Emory University in Atlanta and writes eloquently on the relationship between theology and the economy, the topic of whether ethical behavior also means good business came up. He observed that if "to be ethical means that there are some things one just won't do, then there are times in life where one has tragic choices: to do what is right means giving up a genuine good. This is true for individuals, and I don't see why it isn't true for corporations. Moreover, in a society where everyone is immoral, the person who tries to act ethically will get badly burned. Nevertheless, in a reasonably just society, good action does often enhance business."[2]

But for those times that we just can't count on the good action of participants in the economy, when the belief is that business forces will drive a businessperson to act immorally (or at best amorally) out of fear of getting burned, we end up using regulations to ensure right behavior. Unfortunately, regulations can run amok and sometimes make it impossible for even the most upright and ethical businessperson to navigate through the red tape necessary to cut through before he can actually engage in business. But sometimes, in some instances such as those where the environment is concerned, government intervention is gauged to be among the few ways to keep the ethically behaving businessperson from getting burned for doing the right thing.

Bill Wallace, an environmental consultant, appears in the book *Common Fire: Leading Lives of Commitment in a Complex World.* (The name's a pseudonym given him by the authors.) His company has 17 branches and 350 employees. They work on hazardous waste sites throughout the United States. Wallace believes that regulations are critical in working with hazardous waste. "If the regulations are taken away, people won't do anything," he told the authors. "Now, you may ask, 'Where's the moral fiber of these folks?' but it's 'the tragedy of the commons.' If just one good-hearted person running a foundry on the west end of town says, 'I don't like the fact that we're putting out iron oxide emissions, and we're going to clean this down to the lowest imaginable level,' and the guy on the east end of town decides, To hell with it, I don't care,' then, frankly, the second guy's costs are going to be a lot lower. The first guy can't keep his business competitive if he's the only one who cleans up his act. There have to be regulations that everyone has to meet or nothing is done. And then the question is, What's the level of those regulations, and how safe are they in terms of sustaining the environment? What are their implications with respect to the economics and the market?"[3]

Wallace recognizes the pressures that businesses are under to compete against one another in the marketplace. He also recognizes that once you introduce government regulations into the equation you open a potential Pandora's box unless you carefully consider how extensive those regulations should be. It's an odd balance. Business-people generally cry for less government intervention in the workplace, but then when it comes to issues like those Wallace addresses, those same people want the government to step in claiming that it's not fair if they are getting penalized in the marketplace for doing the right thing, for being good citizens. We want to behave ethically, but we don't want any risk involved. The question then arises about whether the regulations are helping all of us who want to behave ethically to do so, or if what we're trying to do is put the fear of fines and litigation into those people we compete against who don't behave ethically.

What's the difference? Well, let's be clear on one thing first. I'm a strong proponent of regulations that are enacted to protect the environment in a sensible limited way by restricting businesses from doing harm. But I'm also, as you've read in earlier chapters, a firm believer that unless businesspeople understand why certain unethical behaviors should be illegal or prohibited, then the long-term effect of acting out of a fear of litigation is not going to have the desired result of creating a community of businesspeople who are compelled to make ethical decisions on their own. It's only through an understanding of why something is right or wrong and abandoning the once-popular notion that all business is amoral that any change in the behavior of individuals can be hoped for. That's what the stories in this book are all about. By looking at people who grapple with the complexities of a variety of decisions whether they involve money, people, the common good, or all three, we can begin to understand how to think about making tough ethical choices.

After all, there are some things we simply can't rely on government to regulate for us when it comes to environmental issues. That's one of the reasons why it's so important that people in business learn to think about the decisions they make and the impact those decisions will have on various constituencies.

I've already cited research that suggests that companies that pay attention to more than just the economic bottom line outperform those that don't.[4] But that's not the only reason for the importance of weighing out the impact of our decisions on the environment. On a very personal level, when we stop to think about it, continuing to practice business in a way that we know is causing harm has no long-term upside and can only lead to potential harm to us, our businesses, and others in the community. That in and of itself is one reason we should not have to rely totally on government to regulate appropriate behavior.

In a recent discussion with an employee of one of the Environmental Protection Agency's regional offices, he paraphrased a sentiment that he attributed to the great conservationist Aldo Leopold—once you've given your problems over to the government, you've admitted defeat. Leopold also wrote that government "can't do everything, and there are some things it can't do at all. It can't make us decent in our relations with each other, or in our relations with the land we live on, [and] by."[5] But my favorite Leopold observation is this one: "Relegating conservation to government is like relegating virtue to the Sabbath. Turns over to professionals what should be the daily work of amateurs."[6]

Still, while us amateurs can do our best to be environmentally aware in our business dealings, there are times when regulations and government intervention is necessary. The complexity of business sometimes makes it difficult to recognize if and when we're doing damage that we can do something about. And also, sometimes, government regulation is just needed to attempt to protect against behavior that violates what's deemed to be within the realm of acceptable. While I'd love to think, in true libertarian fashion, that if government would just lay off, we'd all be able to behave, I'm not naïve enough to believe that this is true. There are times when even the noblest of intentions go awry.

Righting Wrongs in a Cynical World

How businesspeople act when they find themselves caught operating outside the acceptable boundaries of behavior when it comes to the environment presents an interesting window into how ethical decisions are made to make reparations or set things right. And, in a world in which the public is increasingly cynical about any company's ability to take responsibility for its actions, the decision making becomes even harder when you're found to be doing something wrong.

In 1996, the Colonial Pipeline Company of Atlanta, was found to be in violation of the Clean Water Act when an oil spill occurred from one of its pipelines on the Reedy River in South Carolina. The Associated Press reported that the pipeline rupture killed 35,000 fish and polluted a 23-mile-long stretch of the river.[7] The U.S. Department of Justice finally settled the case with Colonial in early 1999. The company agreed to pay a $7 million fine, to set up procedures to ensure further spills were less likely to occur, and to take out full-page advertisements in three newspapers announcing their responsibility and other aspects of the plea agreement.

The wording of the advertisement, which ran in *The New York Times*, *The Atlanta Journal-Constitution*, and the local Greenville newspaper, cost the company a little more than $100,000 and contained three straightforward paragraphs of copy, the wording of which was agreed to as part of the plea agreement with the Justice Department. The company decided on its own to add the headline across the top of the page: "WE APOLOGIZE!" in boldface capital letters when the advertisement ran on February 25. Rather than run the minimal copy required by the plea deal, Colonial apparently was using the opportunity to apologize to the community as it admitted its responsibility for the oil spill.

The headline took even those who negotiated the deal at the Justice Department by surprise. "When I went down and bought the paper, I said, 'Holy Moses; this is quite impressive,' " says Ruth McQuade who was the government's lead counsel on the Colonial Pipeline case.[8]

The people at Colonial Pipeline who decided to run that headline on the advertisement had to be aware that, given the extent of the damage that had been done by the oil spill, the public who read it might be too cynical to believe its sincerity. But that concern didn't outweigh the company's decision to undertake this act of corporate contrition. Colonial's spokesman, Noel Griese, said shortly after the advertisement ran that the company was attempting to show that it accepted responsibility for the oil spill and the damage it had done.

"We wanted to communicate the message that we had done wrong and that we're going to make an effort to see that this doesn't happen again," Griese says. It appears to be more than just a blatant attempt at getting the best public relations out of a bad situation. McQuade confirmed that the parties at Colonial Pipeline worked to cooperate with the Justice Department from the outset.

It wasn't out of purely altruistic motives that Colonial Pipeline took the action it did. It's important to understand that, once the company knew it was going to be held responsible, there was more of a financial incentive for it to come clean than there had been prior to 1991. If the incident had happened prior to 1991, no matter how much a company wanted to admit fault or apologize to the public, there was more incentive not to do so. "Historically, the U.S. legal system was somewhat hostile to apologies, because apologizing was equivalent to admitting error," said Lynn S. Paine, a management professor at the Harvard Business School. "You were opening this huge Pandora's box of potential liability."

What changed were the federal sentencing guidelines. Starting in 1991, in cases where companies were accused of being in violation of Federal laws, the courts began to take into account whatever efforts management took to prevent misconduct or to take responsibility for its actions when it assessed culpability for the action. The fine assessed to a company which had taken precautions and had accepted responsibility could be significantly less than to one which didn't. "With these new guidelines, you have an incentive rather than a disincentive to apologize," says Professor Paine, who tracks corporate behavior.

Whether it was the change in the sentencing guidelines or just a sense that once it reached a plea agreement it should try to make amends to parts of its constituency, the management at Colonial Pipeline did seem to recognize the importance of thinking through its acts and trying to become a better corporate citizen by showing contrition for what it had done. "The exercise of a corporation trying to put moral emotion into what is essentially a legal statement is a good idea," says Laura L. Nash, director of the Institute for Values-Centered Leadership at Harvard Divinity School. "The word 'apologize' even admits a sense of shame and humility, which is extraordinary for a corporation."

That an apology would be deemed to be a rare act for a corporation that admits to wrongdoing is unfortunate. But perhaps partly because of the encouragement provided in regulatory changes like those in the federal sentencing guidelines, management will begin to let down their guard over fear of admitting wrongdoing when they're clearly in the wrong.

It should tell us something though about the perceived state of corporate honesty that the simple apology in the headline to Colonial's ad, in which it was admitting it had polluted and harmed the environment in a big way, was generally greeted with surprise. One reader of the ad, Pierre Ferrari, a consultant based in Atlanta and a member of the board of directors of Ben & Jerry's ice cream company, tore it out, stapled his business card to it, wrote "To CPC: Accepted" across it, and mailed it to Colonial Pipeline. "It's so rare for a company to admit its wrongdoing and then try to make amends," Mr. Ferrari says. "I thought

the ad was very brave." It was enough of an anomaly in corporate behavior for Mr. Ferrari to sit up and take notice.

Of course there were skeptics to the message. Tochie Blad, an environmental activist who lives in Atlanta and had been following the
Colonial case greeted the ad with less enthusiasm. "The words are
there, but I don't know that they're enough," she says. Blad thinks the
company should have gone further and its apology only becomes valid
if it's followed up by a replacement of the entire pipeline.

It's understandable that someone who was so closely involved in
the problem would skeptically greet anything less than total eradica-
tion of the potential problem. Laura Nash understands the skepticism
when she asks "If the question is, 'Should we instantly exonerate
them?' I'd say no. They have to prove their new reputation." But, she
continues, "there aren't a whole lot of mechanisms for corporate pen-
itence, which is needed to begin to regain trust. And this was a signal
that went straight for the jugular."

The apology in and of itself is indeed not enough. Professor Paine
observes that there's a real danger that public policies that encourage
apologies can also devalue them. "The danger is that they just become
pro forma, insincere and part of your public relations effort. For the
apology to be effective, it has to go along with the corrective action
and repair of the damages that have been done."

In the Colonial Pipeline case, the challenge brought on by thinking ethically about the company's actions and its efforts to make
amends doesn't involve just the company's response, but also the public's response to Colonial's actions. Let's assume that Colonial Pipeline
is truly apologetic for the oil spill and that it is taking responsibility for
it. The challenge then faces others who have some direct or indirect
relationships with the company to decide if they are going to be cynical and unforgiving, or if they are going to accept the apology and
move on with the understanding that Colonial still has a lot to do to
regain public trust.

The challenge then for those constituencies in Colonial's sphere
is to think through whether or how they will continue to hold the

company responsible for its actions while at the same time accepting its apology at face value. When a company's actions affect the common good, then it's not only the management of the company that might be forced into thinking through the ethical implications of its behavior and the responsibility it is going to take, but also the customers, vendors, investors, regulators, neighbors, and others affected in the case.

DOING THE RIGHT THING
BECAUSE IT'S THE RIGHT THING

Once we profess what our attitudes or beliefs are, the actions we take often shed light on how we are to them. In Colonial Pipeline's case, now that the company has paid its fine, made its apology, and laid out what it plans to do to set things right, the actions of the company will be telling about how legitimate its contriteness is.

In Colonial's case, the company was responding to an oil spill for which the Justice Department had determined the company was responsible. But more often a company owner, manager, or employee is faced with what he or she can do about something that they know is harming the environment before any laws—such as the Clean Water Act in Colonial's case—are broken. These decisions might be as simple as starting a company-wide recycling policy or pushing for the company to start using recycled paper products for paper goods in the office.

It's one thing to do the right thing when a hefty fine or jail time is a possibility, quite another when the only motivation is that your conscience is telling you to change. It's particularly difficult to change voluntarily if there's a financial disincentive to do so. How you go through the process of making such a decision—taking into account all the ways it'll effect your business—can say a lot about how you make ethical decisions.

Sometimes people in business find themselves running head-on into an environmental problem caused by their company that they'd never anticipated. When this happens to people who have thought of themselves as environmentalists in their personal lives, the result can be a time of wrenching decision making about how to get personal and business goals realigned. When the decision involves a financial commitment on the part of the company that will cut into profits, it can become even more difficult.

Over a six-year period, entrepreneur Duncan Berry had worked in his off hours to save a 13.5-acre estuary on Vashon Island, now called Fern Cove Sanctuary, off the coast of Seattle. He helped raise three-quarters of a million dollars to set aside the area of natural forest and tidelands, purchased from its fourth-generation owners. "It's a little jewel," says Berry, who considers himself an ardent environmentalist. "And I really felt strongly that it should belong to the Puget Sound community and should not go to one wealthy Microsoft owner."[9]

But in early 1998, Berry quit the board of Fern Cove because of a discovery he made about his industry. Much to his chagrin, he had just learned that the cotton industry was unleashing a "staggering number of toxic chemicals" into the environment. Berry's privately held company, the Apparel Source Inc., makes cotton-knit shirts, selling $50-million worth of them a year. Berry wanted time to study how the 53 million pounds of pesticides and 1.6 billion pounds of synthetic fertilizers applied to cotton grown in the United States each year is not only destroying farmland but is finding its way into food and into cattle feed.[10]

"What I was doing during the day in a very lucrative business was at odds with what I was doing with my life in the off hours," says Berry. The more he studied the issue, the more he found himself confronting what he perceived to be a clear-cut decision. "I had two choices: I could quit, or I could stay at the table and try to effect change," says Berry. He chose the latter.

But even so, after months of research, by spring 1999, Berry had not considered the one move that could have had the most dramatic—and immediate—impact on his company's use of conventional cotton. He and his partner, Randy Clark, could have made the decision to take the lead and shift to using some organic cotton before their customers requested it. But that move would have cut into the company's profits—not erase them, mind you, but certainly reduce them.

So why not do it? Berry's reasoning may sound familiar. It's the line of thinking that people making business decisions take to avoid pursuing strategies that threaten their margins. Companies, as seasoned businesspeople are inclined to argue in situations like this, must guard profits above all. "Our primary mission as a company is to be a profitable organization," Berry says. "I believe very strongly that for this to sustain itself, it has to financially make sense for everybody." For Berry, who operates in a very low-margin business, anything that cuts into the company's profits doesn't make sense.

When he started the business with his partner, Berry never envisioned the Apparel Source as a mouthpiece for environmental change, a company that would tout its devotion to the environment as a selling point to consumers. Yet, "like everyone else," says Berry, "down to the staunchest 'green' customer, I'd said, 'Cotton? Oh yeah, that's great stuff. It's 100 percent natural.' "

When I spoke with him about whether the company would consider making a shift to organic cotton before being able to pass on those costs to customers, Berry did not seem inclined to change his company's ways because of the effect it would have had on his company's profits. But that brings up an interesting question for anyone trying to make a decision to do something about which they feel passionately: Couldn't the fact that the shift would have cost him money make it more worthwhile to do? Indeed, it "speaks of greater commitment if the company can sustain a financial penalty in the short term," says John Elkington, author of *Cannibals with Forks,* and chairman of SustainAbility, a London-based consulting firm that advises companies on economic, environmental, and social issues.

Instead, Berry opted to focus on urging others—namely, one of his major customers—to take the first step. To be fair, that in itself is a bold decision for the company founded in 1994, which ships more than 8 million shirts a year to only two customers, mass retailers Wal-Mart and Target. Based in Kent, Washington, the company employs only 10 full-time workers. To manufacture its shirts, the company works with plants in Los Angeles; Muscle Shoals, Alabama; and Karachi, Pakistan.

Doing business in a way that goes against some strongly held personal values can take a toll on a person's psychic well-being. Berry's recent discovery about the effects of traditional cotton, for example, has left him conflicted about the way he's running the business. "It's been harder to sleep at night since I found out, and it hasn't stopped being harder," he says. "I don't sleep better yet, because I'm not reducing pesticides. It's not visible yet."

Tossing and turning isn't the only barometer of Berry's commitment. He has seriously investigated some of his options. For instance, he learned enough about the cost of organic cotton to understand that he couldn't possibly afford to switch over to it entirely. Where traditional cotton costs 65 cents to 70 cents a pound, organic cotton can cost an additional 50 cents to 60 cents per pound, according to Anderson Warlick, president of Parkdale Mills, the country's largest spinner of cottons. "When you don't use pesticides and herbicides, your yield from the crop is much, much less," says Warlick. "I have to charge more or else it's not worth being in the business."[11]

That kind of price hike can only be sustained by companies like Patagonia, the outdoors clothing maker that shifted to using 100 percent organic cotton in 1995. Because of the company's earthy image, it was also able to pass on some of the increased cost to its customers, raising the price of its cotton garments an average of $2 to $10. "With us being as vocal as we are about the environment, it would have been really hard to continue selling conventional cotton," says Jill Vlahos, director of fabric development at Patagonia, who was involved in the shift to organic cotton.

But unlike Patagonia, which sells $30 T-shirts and $70 jeans directly to its customers through catalogs and company-owned retail stores, the Apparel Source sells some of its shirts to retailers for $3.70. They, in turn, mark them up to $6.99. "Patagonia's an entrenched niche marketer," observes Berry, whereas when he thinks of his end users, "we're talking about Bubba."

Going 100 percent organic, however, was not Berry's only option. Companies like Nike, Gap Inc., and Levi-Strauss have begun to blend a small percentage (typically 1 percent to 6 percent) of organic cotton in with the traditional cotton they use. "That's still a massive amount of organic cotton," says Sandra Marquardt, project coordinator of the Organic Fiber Council, in Richmond, California.

But Marquardt points out that "if it doesn't work for Nike, they don't lose their shirts." For the Apparel Source, shirts *are* their only business. "If we were a general company and this was one little part of some product that we do, then we could be out beating the drums," says Berry's partner, Clark. "But when cotton is in everything we sell, we can't afford to be out beating the drums against what is our total revenue."

But in fact there's no requirement to label the organic cotton percentage in a blended garment, according to Marquardt. "Most companies don't say anything about it," she says. "In some companies they made the decision they were better off not talking about what they were doing because in some cases some consumers might question them about what the other 97 percent is."

It was that very concern, in fact, that Berry and his partner say they encountered when they first approached Target in 1998, suggesting that it introduce a line of blended organic-cotton clothing. If Target would agree to do so, the Apparel Source could then charge the retailer more for its shirts, and Target in turn could charge consumers more, thus preserving Berry's profit margin. "At first they said they didn't even want to talk about it because it's just too explosive," Berry reports.

But Berry says he countered the powers at Target by saying, "Look, this is about choices. If you walked into your grocery store tomorrow, you're going to see a choice of organic produce or nonorganic produce. They're not saying, 'Don't touch that carrot!' If you want to make a difference to the environment, you'll spend a little more. Here's a choice. That's all it is."

It's interesting that Berry can make a passionate argument about why and how Target could make the shift to organic right now in spite of its excuses. Given how strongly he feels, how then does Berry reconcile that with his own decision that it's too risky for his company to make that shift itself?

Especially when, as it turns out, the Apparel Source could afford to make some shift. When I pressed him over breakfast one Sunday morning in Seattle, Berry admitted that on the $6.99 cotton shirts that the Apparel Source sells to Target for $3.70, his company makes a gross profit of 5 percent to 18 percent, depending on where the shirts are manufactured. (The cost is lower on those made by his Pakistani manufacturer.)

If Berry and Clark wanted to, they could earmark a portion of the most profitable of those $6.99 shirts for introducing a blend of 3 percent organic cotton like the one used by some larger companies. The additional cost of using a 3 percent blend would amount to 10 cents a garment, Berry says. If the company ate that cost, it would still be left with a profit, albeit a slender one.

That brings up an interesting dilemma for Berry, and one that others in business might find themselves in at some point. The ethicist W. Michael Hoffman points out that while good ethics in most cases equals good business, "it should not be advanced as the only or even the main reason for doing business ethically. When the crunch comes, when ethics conflicts with the firm's interests, any ethics program that has not already faced up to this possibility is doomed to fail because it will undercut the rationale of the program itself. We should promote business ethics, not because good ethics is good business, but because we are morally required to adopt the moral point of view in all our dealings—and business is no exception. In business, as in all other human endeavors, we must be prepared to pay the costs of ethical behavior."[12]

When push comes to shove, being ethical sometimes means that doing the right thing is not necessarily the best thing for our company. "One thing that the study of ethics has taught us over the past 2,500 years," observes Hoffman, "is that being ethical may on occasion require that we place the interests of others ahead of or at least on par with our own interests. And this implies that the ethical thing to do, the morally right thing to do, may not be in our own self-interest."[13]

Berry could have explored making the shift to an organic-cotton blend on some of the garments made in Pakistan, where his margins are highest. It's theoretically possible, as Berry has acknowledged. But he also admitted that he's never fully explored it.

Had he done so, he might have discovered other advantages—far from certain ones—to surrendering some of his profits. By acting on his own initiative, for example, the company might find itself first in line if Target eventually decided to jump on the blended-cotton bandwagon. The Apparel Source would certainly be better positioned than the retailer's other vendors, who would need time to line up organic suppliers. That readiness could translate into extra orders for Berry. Granted, that's only a prospect, and a long-term one at that. For now there's no guarantee that the company's profits would *ever* regain their current luster.

At breakfast at a restaurant overlooking the Seattle skyline, Berry commented to me that he tries hard to engage in a "right livelihood," which is the fifth step of the eightfold path in Buddhist teachings that advises that we should "earn our living in such a way as to entail no evil consequences. To seek that employment to which we can give our complete enthusiasm and devotion." "That step has got me stuck," Berry told me.

But it didn't seem to me that Berry was stuck. Not really. He has decided that the riskiness of making the shift to an organic-cotton blend before he can pass on the costs of that shift to his customers outweighs the importance of his environmental mission. It's a reflexive part of the business mentality to see profits as untouchable, so it's no wonder that "the bottom line" is frequently pulled out as the ultimate justification for any uncomfortable decision. Nobody's going to fault you for wanting to make money, after all.

But the real question is more delicate: Are there ever times when a business person's personal passion justifies putting profits at substantial risk?

If Berry doesn't want to take that risk, he shouldn't be surprised if Target doesn't want to, either. And he also should understand why customers may not want to foot the bill for his environmental conscience. But if Berry wanted to, he could put his margins where his mouth is, cut into those margins, and change the company's course.

Berry says that his wife, Melany, who worked with him to save the estuary on Vashon Island, places the environmental priority "right up there with our children." A shift to organic cotton, even in a small portion of the garments he makes, might help him sleep better. And then he could more easily answer the question she posed to him when she first learned of the environmental damage the industry is causing: "What do you want your lasting impact to be?"

LEAVING A LEGACY

What do you want your lasting impact to be? That's a provocative question that gets at the heart of how we want to be remembered. If we're to be remembered by our acts, then the decisions we make in business will have a lasting impact on the people we do business with—our employees, vendors, customers, and others—and on the community in which we do business. That impact can be much more far-reaching than we can hope to imagine. My son who teaches high school English in Georgia cherishes the impact he knows he can make if he gets through to just one student in each of his classes. They will in turn go on and touch others and so on and so forth.

The same is true of people in business. It's rare to have the chance to make a real tangible difference, so when the opportunities to address one of your passionate concerns arise, will you be ready to seize the opportunity and do something or will it be simpler to allow the day-to-day operations of your business to distract you from doing what you know needs to be and can be done.

In their book, *The Good Society,* Robert N. Bellah, Richard Madsen, William M. Sullivan, Ann Swidler, and Steven M. Tipton, argue "that if we are going to be the kind of persons we want to be, and live the kind of lives we want to live, then attention and not distraction is essential."[14] They continue: "We cannot be the caring people whom our children need us to be and ignore the world they will live in. We cannot hide from the fact that without effective democratic intervention and institution-building the world economy might accelerate in ways that will tear our lives apart and destroy the environment. Moral discourse is essential in the family; it is also essential in the world. There is no place to hide. 'Distracted from distraction by distraction' is how T.S. Eliot characterized our situation. It is time to pay attention."

That's the real challenge when it comes to ethical decision making in business, whether it involves the environment, an employee, a vendor, or countless other things that affect you and your business day in and day out. For sustained success, you need to find a way to align the concerns you have about money, people, and the common good with those about the bottom-line of your business. It's only through thinking hard about the implications of your decisions on each of these constituencies that you'll ever hope to find a way to reach some sort of balance and comfort.

If you allow distractions to keep you from even thinking about the implications of your decisions—and who can't name at least a dozen distractions right off the top of their head—then you're not making a fully informed decision. The long-term danger is that if you don't address these issues now, increasingly you'll find yourself in a business run in a way you swore you'd never be part of and you'll find you've become a person you never wanted to be. That's the real danger of failing to think through the implications of our decisions. And who wants that to be their legacy?

Afterword: Rules? What Rules?

In an increasingly complex business world, there's a tendency among people to want unambiguous answers to what can only be ambiguous situations. I was reminded of this in a seminar I conducted for graduate students of Harvard Business School and Harvard Divinity School to discuss the language of ethics in business, or, more specifically, how people in business talk about the ethical decisions they make.

At each session, we focused on a different case study and talked about the decisions the various characters in the case made about the ethical dilemmas they faced. What was particularly heartening to me was that here was a group of graduate students as far apart from one another on the physical campus of Harvard as you could possibly be, and, you'd think, as far apart philosophically about what's right and wrong in business behavior. But that wasn't the case. The business school students took as much issue with questionable behavior as the divinity school students did. The wonderful part about the discussions was that these people from different parts of the academic world with vastly different vocational goals brought passion and insight to the exploration of how people in business make difficult choices when facing the needs of competing constituencies. They recognized the difficulty of the decision-making process that occurs when tough choices need to get made that cut across academic lines.

But more than once, when it became clear that no matter what choice a character in one of the cases made, he or she would be giving short shrift to the needs of some group—the customers perhaps, or the environment, or maybe the employees—a student in the seminar would blurt out, "there must be rules for this sort of thing; just tell us the rules."

The rest of the class would then pounce saying what the blurter undoubtedly knew, namely, that there are no universal answers that address all of the tough decisions that get made in business day in and day out, regardless of the scope and scale. Sure, there are some regulations and laws that govern how we behave. And certainly, some industries have rigorous codes of ethics that govern what's acceptable and what's not acceptable behavior.

But there's no universal code of ethics that governs how everyone should behave and everything should be done in the business world. You can set ethical guidelines for specific industries or professions because when you focus that narrowly you can codify something in a way that's meaningful to the practitioners in that field. But business is too vast, too wide in scope, too all-encompassing to come up with a magic list that spells out what should and shouldn't be done in every situation. If it did, then we'd have to find a code that would simultaneously address the ethics of both a Catholic priest who takes confidential confession and a page 6 gossip columnist for one of the daily New York tabloids.

Let's put it this way: As much as it would be comforting to think so, there are no rules set in stone to turn to that you can use to rid yourself of the responsibility of having to think through the ethical decisions you must make in business. There are times where it certainly would be nice to have a list, a guide, something to fall back on when you get embroiled in those nasty choices that make you wonder about your own behavior.

Who wouldn't want to be able to pull out a code of ethics and work down the list:

- Did I steal? Check.
- Did I lie? Check.
- Did I kill someone in the process of making payroll? Check.

But one of the sad by-products of overreliance on industry codes or governmental regulations is that it frees up people caught in the heat of a decision from having to think through the implications of their actions.

That's where the real work gets done, the hard thinking, the coming to terms with the implications of your actions. When you make choices solely on what the law will and won't allow, you free yourself from taking any moral responsibility for your actions. And what fun is that? It's like spending your life as an automaton waiting to be told how to behave, how to make the tough choices that define you, the way you do business, and the way you live your life.

So What Do We Know?

There are no universal rules. Oh sure, there are some things that you can pretty well guess are ethically taboo in any industry. You can safely assume that doing something that you know will kill people or put them at serious risk is not a good thing. It sounds ludicrous to even bring this up. But such issues are rarely as clear-cut when they come up.

Remember the company owner in Chapter 4 who had to decide whether he would sign the audit papers that said he knew of nothing that would financially affect the performance of the company? Well, he signed the papers even though he'd just received a fax telling him that airplanes with engines he'd repaired had been grounded for what the airlines were suggesting was his fault. Sure, those planes were grounded so no one would be at risk on them.

But what about the dozens of engines he repaired in other planes that weren't grounded? Don't we expect him to be concerned about the potential safety of those passengers? He says he didn't worry about that, that that was the concern of the regulators. He was behaving how his advisers suggested he behave so as not to cause concern among his bankers with whom he had significant loans. So, does his concern about the health and survival of his company outweigh the concern about the safety of passengers boarding those planes, regardless of how remote the risk was that engines would fail and cause planes to crash? While he may have ultimately decided to act just as he did, as part of the decision-making process, you'd want to think that the safety issue would come up, wouldn't you?

Short of coming up with yet another version of the mirror test in which you decide if you can look at yourself in the mirror in the morning after you've made the decision you've made (or deciding if you'd do what you'd do if your mother were in the room, or if you had to read about it on tomorrow's front page), there's nothing you can do to replace the thoughtful decision-making process that you'll need to go through to weigh the effects of your decisions.

Okay, stop moaning. I know this sounds like some long, drawn-out arduous process that is about as squishy as month-old zucchini and about as pleasant as working for a boss whose idea of ethics involves a quick call to the lawyers on the cell phone followed by a steamy cup of latté grandé to celebrate his or her high moral fiber (or, more likely, that he dodged an ethical bullet). I'm not talking about that kind of process, that kind of unpleasantness.

What I am talking about can sometimes actually be done relatively quickly, depending on the scope of the decision. And here's where those three spheres—money, people, and the common good—come back into play. After meeting several of the characters in *The Good, the Bad, and Your Business* and sharing the experiences they've been through, you've begun to get a sense of how choices might have been different and so too would outcomes if those characters had weighed the impact of their decision on all three areas that their business choices affect. (If you haven't gotten this, take a minute to thumb back through those earlier chapters, and stop every time the people in the cases are faced with a decision. Then ask yourself: How would I have acted? Or how could the people have chosen differently and what might the outcomes have been then?)

Remember that if you think of money, people, and the common good as three overlapping spheres, a goal is to try to find that place where the three spheres overlap, where your decisions address the needs or concerns of each of those areas. It's no magic solution, but it is a simple and quick process to use when thinking through those decisions you need to make when there's no standard blueprint to follow.

Certainly, there are going to be times when the needs of one sphere are not going to be addressed as fully as those of another. In fact, that's going to be the case more frequently than not. That's where judgment comes into play.

The Simple Truth: You've Got to Think

And that, at some level, is how you get things done in business—you manage, as in partake in the practice of management. That requires thinking and talking about the issues that need addressing to get business done.

Sadly, even in the managing of companies there seems to be a tendency to rely on others to make the tough choices and decisions that need to be made to run a company. Eileen Shapiro, a former McKinsey consultant, author of *Fad Surfing in the Boardroom,* and cofounder of the Hillcrest Group, a consulting firm based in Cambridge, Massachusetts, recognizes the problem inherent in such an arrangement.[1]

"If you grow up in a dysfunctional family in which decisions are being made for you, then you can't make decisions," says Shapiro. "That's essentially what's happening to managers in large companies that are outsourcing thinking to consultants. A junior manager doesn't make a decision until the outside consultant says so. Well, what happens when those junior managers become middle managers? We're breeding a whole generation of managers who can't think."

The concern about people in business increasingly relying on outsiders—whether it be consultants, trade groups, lawyers, or others—is that when faced with incomplete information or struggling to make a choice that may have a serious impact on one of the business' constituencies, the manager might have become skittish about working through any dilemma. Instead, he or she hopes desperately for some *deus ex machina* to fall from the sky providing the answers (a code of ethics, perhaps, or an ethics compliance officer).

"Implicit in my training in business school was that managers make decisions when they don't have complete information," says Shapiro. "That means there's risk. It's scary because you might be wrong. People in organizations typically look to make the decisions that aren't going to get them into trouble. They look for the low-risk decision."

Indeed, that's a sad turn of events for companies that may find their ranks full of managers incapable of making tough calls on their own, whether it's an ethical decision or any decision that falls outside of the documented game plan laid out for the company.

What being a manager comes down to, argues Shapiro, "is a willingness to make decisions, think through the implications, live with the consequences, and learn from mistakes and keep going."

Thinking through the implications of your decisions is precisely what the examples in earlier chapters of this book have stressed. That thinking process involves knowing what questions to ask so that you will be able to make sound decisions.

It sounds simple enough. But you'd be surprised—or, sadder still, maybe you wouldn't—how difficult people in business find making straightforward decisions and talking about issues that involve ethical behavior. When such talk doesn't go on, or you hold back out of fear of talking about it in some way that you fear would make yourself or someone uncomfortable, the real issues get lost and so often too do the most appropriate choices or solutions.

Take the example of a situation where a former Marine was working as a database consultant for a telecommunications company. His desk was placed next to an employee who happened to be devoutly religious and who also found swearing to be offensive, particular when that swearing took the Lord's name in vain.

She complained to her supervisor who in turn brought together the entire group of employees and suggested they read the Ten Commandments to understand why this woman would find such language offensive. (The third commandment: "You shall not take the name of the Lord your God in vain.") The manager thought her approach was innocent enough and perhaps not as offensive as being more direct with the guy who was using the vulgar language that his coworker found so offensive. Simple enough? Yes?

Well, no. As it happens, the former Marine was also a long-time follower of Buddhism and, after he told the manager he was uncomfortable with being told to follow the Ten Commandments and subsequently was fired, he sued the company for religious discrimination.[2]

You might think it foolish that the former Marine brought suit against the company or a mistake for the manager to bring the Ten Commandments into the equation (even though she insisted at trial that she didn't tell employees to "follow" the Ten Commandments, so much as read them to understand how their fellow employee could be so offended). But think of how differently the situation might have turned out if the manager had just been more direct and said to the consultant: "So and so finds your vulgar language offensive. Cut it out." Or words to that effect that left out any reference to religion, or political sensitivity, or watered-down language so as not to risk offending anyone out of the discussion.

Sure, the ex-Marine might have balked at changing his behavior, but then the manager would have been able to decide if she wanted to continue the employment of someone whose behavior other workers found offensive. Contrary to a lot of misguided management gossip, it is still possible to fire employees when they don't do the job you want them to do in the way you want them to do it.

Of course, you'd hope that it wouldn't come to having to fire the ex-Marine, or any employee for that matter. After all, who enjoys firing someone? And who doesn't agree that the mere act of firing can be demoralizing not only for the fired employee but for those who remain?

You'd like to think, wouldn't you, that before it came to that, the parties involved would try to figure out a solution. Oh, perhaps curbing the curse words, for example? Or while you're trying to figure out a solution, maybe moving the ex-Marine's desk as far away from the offended employee as possible until it's clear he's actually capable of losing the expletives from his vocabulary when he's on the job?

But, according to the parties involved, such discussions never occurred. And the whole argument shifted in ways that consumed everyone involved far more than might have happened had the folks involved been direct with one another and stayed focused on the dilemma at hand, namely how do we address the needs of this offended employee in a way that is not offensive to anyone involved or detrimental to anyone's productivity.

KNOWLEDGE IS POWER

Knowledge, as you've read and been told time and time again, is power. And that adage holds true in ethical decision making. In fact, it's at the heart of how to most effectively make such choices.

This makes all kinds of business sense and is a fact not lost on management thinkers as well as ethics experts. John Case, a former colleague of mine at *Inc.* magazine who is now the executive editor of *Harvard Management Update,* a management newsletter, coined the term "open-book management" in an article he wrote in September 1990 to refer to an increasingly popular management method that companies were using to improve business performance.[3] In this method, management shared budgets, income statements, cash-flow analyses, and balance sheets with all employees.

What this said to employees, Case wrote later in his book, *Open-Book Management,* was that "we're all in this business together and we're all accountable to each other for making sure it succeeds."[4] As a result, the "usual sources of mistrust and resentment simply evaporate." Open-book builds trust, Case concluded, because it builds understanding.

It wasn't long before the experts seized on Case's idea as a wonderful window into understanding how disclosing relevant information to employees that was once kept from them can transform the workplace. Such disclosure can help employees understand how the company makes money. And it can have a tremendous effect on their productivity. In turn, employees learn how they can both affect how their company makes money and how they can benefit from it. (Open-book management also frequently includes an employee-ownership component, so the benefit to an employee's pocketbook if the business does well, can be significant.)

Norman Bowie, a business ethics expert, addressed the issue of open-book management in his book *Business Ethics: A Kantian Perspective:*

> The underlying philosophy of open book management is that persons should be treated as responsible autonomous beings. A precondition of such treatment is that employees have the information needed to make responsible decisions. [John] Case calls this "empowerment with brains." . . .
>
> With complete information and the proper incentive, employees behave responsibly without the necessity of layers of supervision.[5]

And in his book, *Human Capital,* Thomas O. Davenport goes further to argue that only by opening its books can a company hope to tap into the human capital that employees bring to a company. His thesis is that employees "are not costs, factors of production, or assets. They are investors in a business, paying in human capital and expecting a return on their investment."[6] To make the connection between human capital investment and strategy, Davenport says, "requires that people understand just how the organization becomes successful."[7]

And lest you think that such understanding doesn't have an impact on the company's bottom line, consider a study conducted by the National Center for Employee Ownership which tracked 50 companies before and after they began practicing open-book management. The findings showed that "revenues of open-book companies grew, on average, 1.66 percent faster than those of their competitors, and 2.2 percent faster if the open-book company also had an employee stock ownership plan."[8]

That's not a huge margin of difference, but it's a difference nonetheless and, when you consider that many open-book managers argue that the real difference comes in a company's profits rather than its revenues, early evidence suggests that, in addition to engaging the workforce in the process of doing business, open-book management does help a company's bottom line. So, here's another striking example that ethical behavior and profits are not necessarily mutually exclusive conceits.

How We Define Ourselves

What's all this got to do with ethical decision making? Well, in a word, everything.

Just as information sharing builds trust among employees and empowers them by helping them understand how business works, the same thing is true about the dilemmas you face in the workplace. The more you can articulate what your options are and how you're trying to weigh the effects of your decision on the various constituencies involved—and the more you can do this in a direct way that avoids jargon and doublespeak ("paradigm shifts!" "it's not without merit!")—the more likely you'll be successful in working through the tough decisions you need to make. No, you won't always please all of the people all of the time, but you will, at the very least, know why it is you're making the decisions you are and so will others involved in the dilemma.

When employees don't understand what a manager is trying to say when they're addressing some issue in the workplace, is it any surprise that the situation quickly deteriorates with employees leaving the room confused at best and filing lawsuits at worst?

When employees don't trust the managers who are empowered with making decisions—or because of their track record of behavior don't believe them to be capable of ethical behavior—is it any wonder that cynicism becomes so pervasive that productivity ultimately drops?

Part of what compels us to behave ethically is that, ultimately, we realize that how we define ourselves—to ourselves and to others—is best articulated in the decisions we make and the way we make those decisions. For better or worse, we show ourselves and the world what we stand for in the choices we make and the actions we take.

There may be no codified set of rules that cuts across every type of business to address every choice you'll have to make, but you can rest assured that on a daily basis, you're going to be faced with making, witness the making, or participate in the making of ethical decisions. These may be grand dilemmas that affect thousands of lives and dozens of communities. Or they may be dilemmas that are smaller in scale. But you'll face them in one form or another on a daily basis and that you can take to the bank.

That being the case, you're going to see a lot of tough decisions being made and sometimes you'll make them yourself. The choices we make that define us then become benchmarks upon which we can measure how to wrestle our way through dilemmas that cross our paths in the future.

We learn as we go along how we feel after having made some of these decisions and we can recalibrate our future behavior if it turns out that the actions we took don't sit right upon further reflection. That's partly what frightens some people about navigating their way through the ethical dilemmas that get in the way of our course. What if we're wrong? What if our choice has devastating outcomes?

Those can indeed be real worries, but what's worse than not making a difficult choice when facing a dilemma is doing nothing at all. It becomes all too easy then to point a finger of blame at the person—perhaps a colleague or a boss—who *did* make the decision. We absolve ourselves from having the moral courage to take responsibility for our actions, because we've lacked the courage to even make a choice. We've failed to do the work necessary to articulate the dilemma facing us and to find possible solutions. Is that any way to run a business?

Remember early on in *The Good, the Bad, and Your Business,* when I brought up the common misconception that ethical behavior always causes pain? While that misconception is off the mark, it's far less distressing than the idea of businesses full of people unwilling to make choices when facing dilemmas. Forget the reason ("there's no payoff," "there's no upside," "why put my ass on the line?").

Instead, imagine a world of commerce where you can't trust the people you're doing business with to engage in ethical behavior. Worse still, imagine that you yourself see no reason to risk making those tough choices as you face them. If you wait long enough, someone else will make the choice and his reputation will be risked. Or, the dilemma will simply go away or be buried deep in the institutional archives along with all those other unfortunate incidents that dare not be spoken about.

Business then limps along. You hire people you can't really trust who know they can't really trust you. You do business with suppliers who fully expect you to try to take advantage of them and they, in turn, do what they can to strike you before you strike them. You don't trust that your customers will be loyal because, well, you're doing everything you can to squeeze out a little more profit, while you cut here and there on the quality assurance program your product once went through.

Forget the gloomily painted scenarios. What really should drive us to do the work necessary to make tough choices when facing ethical dilemmas is that our actions define us in business and in life. When you think through the implications of what you are about to do—or avoid doing—how will you feel about yourself? How would you feel if you were a customer, employee, vendor, neighbor, or other constituency of yours after you acted? And then, even if you feel fine making that decision you've just made, ask yourself when you're in the process of making that decision whether what you've decided to do will do any harm? It's only then that you can hope to do your thoughtful best to do the right thing.

Notes

Chapter 1   It Hurts so Good

1. Edward O. Welles, "Basic Instincts," *Inc.* September 1996: 38.
2. I was told of this incident by Sharon Daloz Parks, one of the co-authors with Thomas R. Piper and Mary C. Gentile of *Can Ethics Be Taught: Perspectives, Challenges, and Approaches at Harvard Business School* (Boston: Harvard Business School Press, 1993).
3. *Hoover's Handbook of American Business* (Hoover's Inc., 1998). For good insight into Johnson & Johnson's reaction to the Tylenol case and how its actions grew out of a reliance on the company's corporate credo written in 1943, see James C. Collins and Jerry I. Porras, *Built to Last: Successful Habits of Visionary Companies* (New York: HarperBusiness, 1994), pp. 58–61.
4. James C. Collins and Jerry I. Porras, *Built to Last: Successful Habits of Visionary Companies* (New York: HarperBusiness, 1994), p. 58.
5. It was in conversations with Richard Unsworth, the retired dean of the chapel at Smith College, that I came upon the use of "ethos" in this context. He cited the work of Paul Lehmann who taught at Union Theological Seminary and the Harvard Divinity School and used the term "ethos" in this way in his lectures and in his book, *Ethics in a Christian Context* (New York: Harper and Row, 1963).

6. These figures come from David Condon, a lawyer with Edgewater Holdings, an insurer in Chicago, who since 1990 has been tracking the number of wrongful termination suits filed in the United States. Also see Jeffrey L. Seglin, "In Dismissals, Silence Has Its Perils," *The New York Times,* 18 October 1998, Section 3, p. 4. And see Walter K. Olson, *The Excuse Factory: How Employment Law is Paralyzing the American Workplace* (New York: The Free Press, 1997).

7. John Elkington, *Cannibals with Forks: The Triple Bottom Line of 21st Century Business* (Stony Creek, Connecticut: New Society Publishers, 1998). While Elkington and others in the sustainability movement use "triple bottom line" to reflect an economic, environmental, and social bottom line, others use the phrase "three bottom lines" to refer to profit, operating cash flow, and return on assets—all financial measures.

8. John P. Kotter and James L. Heskett, *Corporate Culture and Performance* (New York: The Free Press, 1992), p. 11.

Chapter 2   When Payrolls Keep Us Up at Night

1. These figures are from Challenger, Gray & Christmas, the Chicago-based outplacement firm that tracks these numbers regularly. It's cited in Jeffrey L. Seglin, "The 1998 *Inc.*/Gallup Survey: Americans at Work," *Inc.,* June 1998: 91.

2. Carol Gilligan, *In a Different Voice: Psychological Theory and Women's Development* (Cambridge, Massachusetts: Harvard University Press, 1982), pp. 25–31.

3. Jeffrey L. Seglin, "Hot Strategy: 'Be Unprofitable for a Long Time'," *Inc.,* September 1997: 32. In this interview with Jeffrey Bezos, founder and CEO of amazon.com, the online bookseller, in response to a question about a statement in its prospectus for a public offering that the company "will incur substantial losses for the foreseeable future," he responds: "We're going to be unprofitable for a long time. And that's our strategy."

4. David Murray, *Ethics in Organizations* (London: Kogan Page Limited, 1997), p. 113.

5. This figure is cited all over the place in small business financing literature, from manuals to handbooks to web sites like that of Bank-Boston at www.bankboston.com/business/resources/cashflow.asp, "How Healthy Is Your Company's Cash Flow?" According to Bruce Phillips, an economist with the Small Business Administration in an e-mail on February 4, 1999, "Old myths die hard deaths. I have been with SBA since 1979, and have invested 20 years in this kind of research. I have absolutely no idea where that 90 percent figure comes from, but "it ain't here." It is also wrong. Of small firms that dissolve (about 1 in 6 actually fail—leave unpaid debts), most do so because of internal reasons—inability to manage people, lack of a business plan, and, yes, undercapitalization. Some fail because they do not offer a competitive product or service, or because of external reasons—like the appearance of a Home Depot or a recession. I do not know the percentage of small firms that fail because of undercapitalization—or the inability to raise capital to expand. But it is nowhere near 90 percent from the few surveys that I have seen."

6. James L. Bildner, "Hitting the Wall," *Inc.*, July 1995: 21.

7. Susan Hansen, "Soaring Video Chain Crashes to Earth," *Inc.*, November 1998: 23.

8. Phaedra Hise, "Boston Ad Agency Finds Cost of Doing Business Doesn't Add Up," *Inc.*, February 1997: 25.

9. Tom Fudge, "Flapjack Chain Runs Out of Dough," *Inc.*, October 1997: 25.

10. Barry Keesan, "My Smartest Mistakes," *Fast Company*, October 1997.

11. Norm Brodsky, "Paying for Growth," *Inc.*, October 1996: 29.

12. Jeffrey L. Seglin, "Always a Payroll to Meet," *Inc.*, January 1998. The case study told here was originally told in a different form in this article in *Inc.* magazine. Unless noted otherwise, while the

telling of the story is new, the quotes from the subjects in this case are draw from this article.

13. From "Readers' Debate: 'Does Your Word Mean Anything?'" in "Brother, Can You Spare 30 Cents on the Dollar?" *Inc.*, April 1998: 47.

14. Edwin Hartman, *Organizational Ethics and the Good Life* (New York: Oxford University Press, 1996), pp. 99–100.

15. Brodsky, "Paying for Growth," *Inc.*, October 1996: 29.

16. From "Readers' Debate: 'Does Your Word Mean Anything?'" in "Brother, Can You Spare 30 Cents on the Dollar?" *Inc.*, April 1998: 47.

17. James C. Collins and Jerry I. Porras, *Built to Last: Successful Habits of Visionary Companies* (New York: HarperBusiness, 1994), p. 73.

18. Collins and Porras, p. 71.

19. Abraham H. Maslow, "The Enlightened Manager's Guidebook," *Inc.*, October 1998. Adapted from *Maslow on Management* by Abraham H. Maslow, with Deborah Stephens and Gary Heil (New York: John Wiley & Sons, 1998).

Chapter 3   Just Because It's Legal, Is It Right?

1. Robert A. Mamis, "Why Bankruptcy Works," *Inc.*, October 1996: 39.

2. "Bankruptcies Break Another Record During 12-Month Period Ending Sept.," November 23, 1998. Posted on American Bankruptcy web site at www.abiworld.org.

3. Interview by the author with Judge James A. Goodman, January 1998.

4. In what seems to be a classic example of what goes around comes around, Boston Chicken filed for chapter 11 bankruptcy protection in October 1998. By the time of the filing, George Naddaff

was not with the management team running the company. See Mike Hofman, "Boston Chicken Files Ch. 11 as Troubles Come Home to Roost," Inc. Online, October 7, 1998.

5. Joshua Hyatt, "The Next Big Thing," *Inc.*, November 1995: 62.

6. Jeffrey L. Seglin, "Brother, Can You Spare 30 Cents on the Dollar?" *Inc.*, April 1998. The case study told here was originally told in a different form in this article in *Inc.* magazine. Unless noted otherwise, while the telling of the story is new, the quotes from the subjects in this case are drawn from this article.

7. Shaun Schafer, "CFS still looks for buyers." *Tulsa World*, January 27, 1999 and Julie Bryant, "Founder of CFS won't be in office," January 22, 1999. Also: Clytie Bunyan and Andy Parsons, "You've Got No Job, E-Mail Says," *The Daily Oklahoman*, June 24, 1999.

8. From "Readers' Debate: Is It 'Right' to Go Bankrupt?" in "Would You Lie to Save Your Company? *Inc.*, July 1998: 53.

9. Interview by the author with Judge James A. Goodman, January 1998.

10. From "Readers' Debate: Is It 'Right' to Go Bankrupt?" in "Would You Lie to Save Your Company? *Inc.*, July 1998: 53.

11. Robert A. Mamis, "Why Bankruptcy Works," *Inc.*, October 1996: 39.

12. From "Readers' Debate: Is It 'Right' to Go Bankrupt?" in "Would You Lie to Save Your Company? *Inc.*, July 1998: 53.

13. From "Readers' Debate: Is It 'Right' to Go Bankrupt?" in "Would You Lie to Save Your Company? *Inc.*, July 1998: 53.

14. Joshua Hyatt, "The Next Big Thing," *Inc.*, November 1995: 62.

Chapter 4   How to Make a Decision When You Don't Know Enough

1. Kenneth R. Andrews, "Ethics in Practice," *Harvard Business Review*, September 1989/October 1989: 99.

2. Rushworth M. Kidder, *How Good People Make Tough Choices: Resolving the Dilemmas of Ethical Living* (New York: William Morrow, 1995), p. 186.

3. William James, *Pragmatism* (Indianapolis: Hackett Publishing Company, 1981). James' book was first published in 1907 and was based on a series of lectures he had delivered in Boston in 1906. His notion that people exist with characteristics of "tough-mindedness" as well as "tender-mindedness" is clearly laid out in this work. He goes further to observe that the "tough think of the tender as sentimentalists and soft-heads. The tender feel the tough to be unrefined, callous, or brutal" (p. 11). As he points out, however, few people are "pure and simple" tender- or tough-minded people.

4. Norman R. Augustine, "Reaping the returns of ethical acts: An American imperative," *Vital Speeches of the Day,* August 15, 1997: Vol. 63, No. 21: 658–660. Address given by Augustine to the School of Business Administration, Georgetown University, Washington, D.C., May 24, 1997. I've also heard the rule that you might consider something unethical in business if you'd not want to read about it on the front page of *The New York Times* or *The Wall Street Journal* attributed to Berkshire Hathaway CEO Warren Buffett.

5. Peter F. Drucker, *Management Challenges for the 21st Century* (New York: HarperBusiness, 1999), p. 175.

6. Laura L. Nash, "Ethics Without the Sermon," *Harvard Business Review,* November 1981/December 1981: 79.

7. Drucker, p. 176.

8. *Hoover's Handbook of American Business* (Hoover's Inc., 1998).

9. Laura L. Nash, *Good Intentions Aside: A Manager's Guide to Resolving Ethical Problems* (Boston: Harvard Business School Press, 1990), p. 39.

10. For good insight into Johnson & Johnson's reaction to the Tylenol case and how its actions grew out of a reliance on the company's corporate credo written in 1943, see James C. Collins and Jerry

I. Porras, *Built to Last: Successful Habits of Visionary Companies* (New York: HarperBusiness, 1994), pp. 58–61.

11. Nash, *Good Intentions Aside,* p. 40.

12. Jeffrey L. Seglin, "Would You Lie to Save Your Company?" *Inc.,* July 1998. The case study told here was originally told in a different form in this article in *Inc.* magazine. Unless noted otherwise, while the telling of the story is new, the quotes from the subjects in this case are drawn from this article.

13. From "Readers' Debate: Was CEO 'Morally Vacant' to Ignore Potential Loss of Life?" in "True Lies," *Inc.,* Special *Inc.* 500 issue, 1998: 136.

14. Andrews, "Ethics in Practice," p. 99.

15. "Readers' Debate: Was CEO 'Morally Vacant' to Ignore Potential Loss of Life?" p. 136.

16. Ibid.

17. Ibid.

18. Andrews, "Ethics in Practice," p. 99.

Chapter 5   *It's Enough to Drive You to Drink*

1. Stephen L. Carter, *Civility: Manners, Morals, and the Etiquette of Democracy* (New York: Basic Books, 1998), pp. 181–182.

2. Jeffrey L. Seglin, "The Happiest Workers in the World," *Inc.,* State of Small Business issue, 1996: 62.

3. Laura L. Nash, *Good Intentions Aside: A Manager's Guide to Resolving Ethical Problems* (Boston: HBS Press, 1993), p. 98.

4. Kenneth E. Goodpaster, "Note on the Corporation As a Moral Environment," in *Ethics in Practice: Managing the Moral Corporation,* edited by Kenneth R. Andrews (Boston: HBS Press, 1989), p. 93.

5. Goodpaster, p. 93.

6. Paul F. Camenisch, "A Religious Approach to Business Ethics," in *Perspectives in Business Ethics,* edited by Laura Pincus Hartman (Chicago: Irwin McGraw-Hill, 1998), pp. 232–233.

7. Rabindra N. Kanungo and Manuel Mendonca, *Ethical Dimensions of Leadership* (Thousand Oaks, CA: Sage Publications, 1996), p. 38.

8. Jeffrey L. Seglin, "The Savior Complex," *Inc.,* February 1999. The case study told here was originally told in a different form in this article in *Inc.* magazine. Unless noted otherwise, while the telling of the story is new, the quotes from the subjects in this case are drawn from this article. It is used with permission of the publisher.

9. Laura L. Nash, *Believers in Business* (Nashville: Thomas Nelson Publishers, 1994), pp. 156–157.

10. Joseph L. Badaracco, Jr., *Defining Moments: When Managers Must Choose between Right and Right* (Boston: HBS Press, 1997), p. 45.

11. Irvin D. Yalom, *Love's Executioner and Other Tales of Psychotherapy* (New York: HarperPerennial, 1989), p. 8.

12. The International EAP Association publishes a great deal of good material on employee assistance programs. Its Web site is http://www.eap-association.com; address is: 2101 Wilson Boulevard, Suite 500, Arlington, Virginia 22201, 703-522-6272, fax: 703-522-4585.

13. Interview with Jeffrey Zeizel, October 1998.

14. From "Readers' Debate: Did CEO Place the Company's Reputation in Jeopardy by Helping a Troubled Employee?" published with "It's Not That Easy Going Green," *Inc.,* May 1999: 28.

15. Laura L. Nash, *Believers in Business* (Nashville: Thomas Nelson Publishers, 1994), pp. 157–158.

Chapter 6 Doing the Right Thing for Legal Reasons

1. Linda Klebe Trevino, Gary R. Weaver, David G. Gibson, and Barbara Ley Toffler, "Managing Ethics and Legal Compliance: What Works and What Hurts," *California Management Review,* Winter 1999: 135.

2. Joseph L. Badaracco, Jr. and Allen P. Web, "Business Ethics: A View from the Trenches," *California Management Review,* Winter 1995: 24.

3. Philip K. Howard, *The Death of Common Sense: How Law Is Suffocating America* (New York: Random House, 1994), p. 175.

4. Howard, p. 185.

5. Howard, p. 174.

6. Howard, p. 173.

7. "SHRM Reference Checking Survey," conducted July 1998 by the Society for Human Resource Management, 1800 Duke Street, Alexandria, Virginia 22314, 703-548-3440; http://www.shrm .org.

8. Jeffrey L. Seglin, "Too Much Ado About Giving References," *The New York Times,* February 21, 1999, Section 3; p. 4.

9. David W. Arnesen, C. Patrick Fleenor, and Marlin Blizinsky, "Name, Rank, and Serial Number? The Dilemma of Reference Checks," *Business Horizons,* July 17, 1998, p. 71 ff.

10. R.L. Paetzold and S.L. Willborn, "Employer (Ir)rationality and the Demise of Employment References," *American Business Law Journal,* May 1992, pp. 123–142.

11. Seglin, "Too Much Ado About Giving References," *The New York Times,* February 21, 1999, Section 3; p. 4.

12. "California Court Finds School Districts Negligent in Providing Recommendations," *Human Resources Report* (BNA, Inc.), February 3, 1997. The case citation is Randi W.v. Muroc Joint Unified School District, Calif SuperCt, No. S051441, 1/27/97). There was also the case involving singer Diana Ross in which she

wrote a letter stating "If I let an employee go, it's because either their work or their personal habits are not acceptable to me. I do not recommend these people. In fact, if you hear from these people, and they use my name as a reference, I wish to be contacted." A former executive assistant to Ms. Ross brought a claim against her, alleging that she falsely asserted she had been fired. While the District Court ruled that Ms. Ross' letter was not libelous, the Federal Court of Appeals agree with the former employee arguing that the "Ross letter could be interpreted by an average reader as insinuating" that she "was discharged for lack of professional competence," "especially because of the denial of a recommendation." (As reported in "Recent Cases," *Entertainment Law Reporter,* March 1986.)

13. Interview with author, February 1999.

14. Seglin, "Too Much Ado About Giving References," *The New York Times,* February 21, 1999, Section 3; p. 4.

15. Pierre Mornell, *45 Effective Ways for Hiring Smart: How to Predict the Winners and Losers in the Incredibly Expensive People-Reading Game* (Berkeley, CA: Ten Speed Press, 1998), p. 124.

16. Seglin, "Too Much Ado About Giving References," *The New York Times,* February 21, 1999, Section 3; p. 4.

17. Simon J. Nadel and Jeffrey Goldfarb, "Some States Give Immunity to Employers Providing References, But Concerns Linger," *Human Resources Report* (BNA, Inc.), May 27, 1996.

18. Stuart Silverstein, "Fear of Lawsuits Spurs the Birth of New Industry," *Los Angeles Times,* June 27, 1998: part A; p. 1.

19. David Condon since 1990 has been tracking the number of wrongful termination suits filed in the United States.

20. Interview with author, July 1998.

21. Jeffrey L. Seglin, "In Dismissals, Silence Has Its Perils," *The New York Times,* 18 October 1998, Section 3, p. 4. And see Walter K. Olson, *The Excuse Factory: How Employment Law Is Paralyzing the American Workplace* (New York: The Free Press, 1997).

22. Interview with author, July 1998.

23. Interview with author, July 1998. And Seglin, "In Dismissals, Silence Has Its Perils," *The New York Times,* 18 October 1998, Section 3, p. 4.

24. Seglin, "In Dismissals, Silence Has Its Perils," *The New York Times,* 18 October 1998, Section 3, p. 4.

25. Interview with author, July 1998. And Seglin, "In Dismissals, Silence Has Its Perils," *The New York Times,* 18 October 1998, Section 3, p. 4.

26. Interview with author, July 1998.

27. June Kronholz and Alejandro Bodipo-Memba, "What if It Were a Corporate Executive and an Intern?" *The Wall Street Journal,* September 11, 1998, p. B1.

28. Jeffrey L. Seglin, "Between Consenting Co-Workers," *The New York Times,* September 20, 1998, Section 3; p. 4; Column 2.

29. "1998 Workplace Romance Survey," Society for Human Resources Management, January 1998.

30. Seglin, "Between Consenting Co-Workers," *The New York Times,* September 20, 1998, Section 3; p. 4; Column 2.

31. Heather Pauly, "Sex and the Workplace," *Chicago Sun-Times,* August 26, 1998, p. 6. Also Seglin, "Between Consenting Co-Workers," *The New York Times,* September 20, 1998, Section 3; p. 4; Column 2.

32. Seglin, "Between Consenting Co-Workers," *The New York Times,* September 20, 1998, Section 3; p. 4; Column 2.

33. Seglin, "Between Consenting Co-Workers," *The New York Times*, September 20, 1998, Section 3; p. 4; Column 2.

34. Howard, p. 174.

35. Interview with author, July 1998. And Seglin, "In Dismissals, Silence Has Its Perils," *The New York Times*, 18 October 1998, Section 3, p. 4.

Chapter 7   Where Do We Draw the Lines?

1. Jeffrey L. Seglin, "Diss Connection," *Inc. Technology*, March 15, 1999, p. 31.

2. Milton Friedman, "The Social Responsibility of a Business Is to Increase Its Profits," *New York Times Magazine*, September 3, 1970.

3. Alfred Carr, "Is Business Bluffing Ethical?" *The New York Times*, March 9, 1967.

4. John Morse, "The Missing Link between Virtue Theory and Business Ethics," *Journal of Applied Philosophy*, Vol. 16, No. 1, 1999: 51.

5. Morse, pp. 56–57.

6. Aristotle, *The Basic Works of Aristotle*, Richard McKeon, Ed. (New York: Random House, 1941), *Politica*, translated by Benjamin Jowett, p. 1130.

7. Margaret J. Wheatley and Myron Kellner-Rogers, *A Simpler Way* (San Francisco: Berrett-Kohler, 1999), p. 62.

8. Alan Briskin, *The Stirring of Soul in the Workplace* (San Francisco: Berrett-Kohler, 1998), p. 229.

9. Ralph T. King, Jr., "Lehman Analyst's Misdirected E-mail Offers a Glimpse into Office Politics," *The Wall Street Journal*, December 4, 1998.

10. "The Boss Legally Can Tune into High-Tech Conversations," *The Tampa Tribune*, February 19, 1995, p. 7.

11. Dana Hawkins, "Office Politics in the Electronic Age," *U.S. News & World Report,* March 22, 1999, pp. 59–61.

12. A personal disclosure: Before she went on to law school, Beth Gunn worked for a short time at the same magazine where I was an editor, which is where I first learned of this story.

13. Hawkins, "Office Politics in the Electronic Age," *U.S. News & World Report,* March 22, 1999, p. 60.

14. *Goldhirsh Group, Inc. v. Alpert,* 107 F.3d 105, 109–110 (2d Cir. 1997).

15. Margaret J. Wheatley and Myron Kellner-Rogers, *A Simpler Way* (San Francisco: Berrett-Kohler, 1999), p. 63.

16. Jeffrey L. Seglin, "Saving a Life but Crossing a Line," *The New York Times,* November 15, 1998, Section 3; p. 4; Column 2.

17. Ellen Goodman, "When the Gift of Life Goes Beyond Family," *The Boston Globe,* October 15, 1998, p. A19.

18. Patricia Davis, "Fringe Benefit for the Boss: A New Life; Worker Lends a Hand by Giving a Kidney," *The Washington Post,* October 5, 1998, p. A1.

19. Unless otherwise noted, the quotes relating to the Nancy Nearing and Art Helms story are from Jeffrey L. Seglin, "Saving A Life but Crossing a Line," *The New York Times,* November 15, 1998, Section 3; p. 4; Column 2.

20. Robert C. Solomon, *Ethics and Excellence: Cooperation and Integrity in Business* (New York: Oxford University Press, 1993), pp. 226–227.

21. Solomon, *Ethics and Excellence: Cooperation and Integrity in Business* (New York: Oxford University Press, 1993), pp. 248–249.

22. Solomon, *Ethics and Excellence: Cooperation and Integrity in Business* (New York: Oxford University Press, 1993), pp. 248–249.

23. E-mail from Nancy Nearing to author on December 14, 1998.

24. Laurent A. Parks Daloz, Cheryl H. Keen, James P. Keen, and Sharon Daloz Parks, *Common Fire: Leading Lives of Commitment in a Complex World* (Boston: Beacon Press, 1996), p. 12.

25. E-mail from Nancy Nearing to author on December 14, 1998.

26. Jon K. Rust, Letter to the Editor, *The New York Times,* November 29, 1998, Section 3; p. 6; Column 4.

27. Laurent A. Parks Daloz, Cheryl H. Keen, James P. Keen, and Sharon Daloz Parks, *Common Fire: Leading Lives of Commitment in a Complex World* (Boston: Beacon Press, 1996), p. 14.

28. Robert N. Bellah, Richard Madsen, William M. Sullivan, Ann Swidler, and Steven M. Tipton, *Habits of the Heart: Individualism and Commitment in American Life* (New York: Harper-Perennial, 1985), pp. 45–46.

29. Interview with author November 1998.

Chapter 8   True Lies

1. Ethics panel discussion at the Mint Theater production of "The Voysey Inheritance," New York, June 13, 1999.

2. Sissela Bok, *Lying: Moral Choice in Public and Private Life* (New York: Pantheon, 1978), p. 31.

3. Max L. Stackhouse, "The Ten Commandments: Economic Implications," in *On Moral Business: Classical and Contemporary Resources for Ethics in Economic Life,* edited by Max L. Stackhouse, Dennis P. McCann, and Shirley J. Roels with Preston Williams (Michigan: William B. Eerdmans, 1995), p. 61.

4. Jeffrey L. Seglin, "Bosses Beware When Bending the Truth," *The New York Times,* December 20, 1998, Section 3; p. 4; Column 1.

5. "Cheating and Succeeding: Record Numbers of Top High School Students Take Ethical Shortcuts," Annual Survey Results Database, www.eci-whoswho.com/highschool/annualsurveys/29.shtml.

6. Robert R. Taylor and Kristin O. Prien, "Preventing Employee Theft: A Behavioral Approach," *Business Perspectives,* June 1998, Vol. 10, No. 4, p. 9.

7. Seglin, "Bosses Beware When Bending the Truth," p. 4.

8. Roy J. Lewicki and Robert J. Robinson, "Ethical and Unethical Bargaining Tactics: An Empirical Study," *Journal of Business Ethics,* 18: 211–228, 1998. Also Jeff Grabmeier, "MBA Students Have Clear Ideas of What Is Ethical in Negotiations," Ohio State University Newsfeatures, September 28, 1998.

9. Sissela Bok, *Lying: Moral Choice in Public and Private Life* (New York: Pantheon, 1978), p. 31.

10. Seglin, "Bosses Beware When Bending the Truth," p. 4.

11. Sissela Bok, *Lying: Moral Choice in Public and Private Life* (New York: Pantheon, 1978), p. 79.

12. Seglin, "Bosses Beware When Bending the Truth," p. 4.

13. Brad Blanton, *Radical Honesty* (New York: Dell, 1996), p. xli.

14. Robert Solomon, "Is It Ever Right to Lie? (On Truth in Advertising)" in *Perspectives in Business Ethics,* edited by Laura Pincus Hartman (Chicago: Irwin McGraw-Hill, 1998), p. 567.

15. A version of the story involving the survey of *Inc.* 500 CEOs who said that bootstrapping a business required some "unsavory business practices" appeared first as a *Black and White* business ethics column I wrote for the magazine. That story, which is adapted with permission for this chapter, appeared originally as: "True Lies," *Inc., Inc.* 500 special issue 1998. The quotes from the *Inc.* 500 CEOs who answered are from that article.

16. In October 1998, Molina left Let's Talk Cellular & Wireless. See "Who's News," *The Wall Street Journal,* October 12, 1998, Section B; p. 5, Col. 3.

17. From "Readers' Debate: Does stretching the truth set a 'dangerous precedent' for a start-up CEO?" in "The Savior Complex," *Inc.,* February 1999: 66.

18. Stephen L. Carter, *Integrity* (New York: HarperPerennial, 1996), p. 56.

19. Sissela Bok, *Lying: Moral Choice in Public and Private Life* (New York: Pantheon, 1978), p. xxi.

20. Stephen L. Carter, *Integrity* (New York: HarperPerennial, 1996), p. 38.

21. From "Readers' Debate: Does stretching the truth set a 'dangerous precedent' for a start-up CEO?" *Inc.*, February, 1999: 66.

22. Sissela Bok, *Lying: Moral Choice in Public and Private Life* (New York: Pantheon, 1978), p. 31.

Chapter 9   Spies Like Us

1. Daniel Eisenberg, "Eyeing the Competition," *Time,* March 22, 1999: 58.

2. Gregg Krupa, "Raytheon Unit Settles Industrial-spying Allegations," *The Boston Globe,* May 13, 1999: D3.

3. Edward O. Welles, "Blind Ambition," *Inc.,* November 1989: 94.

4. Candace L. Preston, "Out-of-Work Spies Find New Niche in Corporate Espionage," *Business First-Columbus,* November 28, 1997: 27.

5. Interview between Richard J. Heffernan and author, January 1999. Also see *Trends in Intellectual Property Loss Survey Report* by Dan T. Swartwood and Richard J. Heffernan, sponsored by the American Society for Industrial Security, 1625 Prince Street, Alexandria, Virginia 22314, 703-522-5800.

6. Interview between Patrick J. Gnazzo and author, January 1999.

7. Ira Winkler, "Corporate Espionage," excerpted in *Inc.,* June 1997: 91.

8. Interview between Christopher Bogan and author, January 1999.

9. Interview between Tom Peters and author, January 1999.

10. Interview between Patrick J. Gnazzo and author, January 1999.

11. Melody Petersen, "Lawsuits by Rivals Accuse Textile Maker of Corporate Espionage," *The New York Times,* October 13, 1998: C1.

12. "Milliken & Company Statement in Response to Allegations by Johnston Industries," Press Statement, December 31, 1998, Richard Dillard, Director, Public Affairs, Milliken & Company.

13. Quotes from various parties about the Milliken case, unless otherwise noted, come from: Jeffrey L. Seglin, "Boundaries to Stealing All Those Bright Ideas," *The New York Times,* January 17, 1999: Section 3; p. 6.

14. Christopher E. Bogan and Michael J. English, *Benchmarking for Best Practices: Winning Through Innovative Adaptation* (New York: McGraw-Hill, 1994), p. 24.

15. Tom Peters and Nancy Austin, *A Passion for Excellence: The Leadership Difference* (New York: Random House, 1985), pp. 14–17.

16. Interview between Tom Peters and author, January 1999.

Chapter 10   Whole Earth Policy

1. Paul Hawken, *The Ecology of Commerce* (New York: Harper-Business, 1993), p. 127.

2. E-mail exchange with Jon Gunnemann, April 22, 1999.

3. Laurent A. Parks Daloz, Cheryl H. Keen, James P. Keen, and Sharon Daloz Parks, *Common Fire: Leading Lives of Commitment in a Complex World* (Boston: Beacon Press, 1996), pp. 20–21.

4. See John Kotter and James Heskett, *Corporate Culture and Performance* (New York: The Free Press, 1992).

5. Aldo Leopold, from his essay "Conservation," written around 1942, provided by Curt Meine, the coeditor of *The Essential*

Aldo Leopold: Quotations and Commentaries, forthcoming from the University of Wisconsin Press.

6. Aldo Leopold. Unpublished undated lecture notes, provided by Curt Meine, the coeditor of *The Essential Aldo Leopold: Quotations and Commentaries,* forthcoming from the University of Wisconsin Press.

7. "Company Runs Ads Apologizing for S.C. Spill," The Associated Press State & Local Wire, March 2, 1999.

8. Quotes from the parties involved in the Colonial Pipeline case, unless otherwise noted, come from: Jeffrey L. Seglin, "A Safer World for Corporate Mea Culpas," *The New York Times,* March 21, 1999, Section 3; p. 4; Column 2.

9. Jeffrey L. Seglin, "It's Not That Easy Going Green," *Inc.,* May 1999. The case study told here was originally told in a different form in this article in *Inc.* magazine. Unless noted otherwise, while the telling of the story is new, the quotes from the subjects in this case are drawn from this article. It is used with permission of the publisher.

10. These figures come from the *Organic Cotton Directory 1998–99,* produced by the Organic Trade Association's Fiber Council (P.O. Box 1078, Greenfield, MA 01302, ofc@igc.org) and the Pesticide Action Network (49 Powell Street, Suite 500, San Francisco, CA 94102, panna@panna.org, www.panna.org/panna).

11. Interview between author and Warlick, January 1999.

12. W. Michael Hoffman, "Business and Environmental Ethics," in *Perspectives in Business Ethics,* edited by Laura Pincus Hartman (Chicago: Irwin McGraw-Hill, 1998), pp. 700–701.

13. W. Michael Hoffman, "Business and Environmental Ethics," pp. 700–701.

14. Robert N. Bellah, Richard Madsen, William M. Sullivan, Ann Swidler, and Steven M. Tipton, *The Good Society* (New York: Alfred A. Knopf, 1991), pp. 275–276. The T.S. Eliot poem referenced is "Burnt Norton."

Afterword: Rules? What Rules?

1. Jeffrey L. Seglin, "You Can Lead a Manager to Order, But You Can't Make Him Think," *Inc.,* December 1996: 30. Eileen Shapiro is also the author of two books on the faddish nature of management and the damage that it does to good decision-making skills in the workplace: *Fad Surfing in the Boardroom: Managing in the Age of Instant Answers* (Boston: Perseus, 1997) and *The Seven Deadly Sins of Business: Freeing the Corporate Mind from Doom-Loop Thinking* (London: Capstone, 1998). Each book features an appendix with her own version of "The Devil's Dictionary," which is a biting dictionary of jargon, acronyms, and other stuff of management fads.

2. At the time this book went to press, the case had gone through one trial and was in appeal. In the first trial, the jury found that the manager interfered with the consultant's contract but did not discriminate against him on religious grounds. Both sides appealed the finding. See Jeffrey L. Seglin, "Regulating Religious Life In the Office," *The New York Times,* Section 3; p. 4, for the column I wrote about the case.

3. John Case, "The Open-Book Managers," *Inc.,* September 1990: 104.

4. John Case, *Open-Book Management* (New York: HarperBusiness, 1996), p. 46.

5. Norman E. Bowie, *Business Ethics: A Kantian Perspective* (Oxford: Blackwell Publishers, 1999), p. 54.

6. Thomas O. Davenport, *Human Capital: What It Is and Why People Invest It* (San Francisco: Jossey-Bass, 1999), p. xii.

7. Davenport, p. 101.

8. George Gendron, "The Numbers on Open-Book Management," *Inc.,* June 1998: 11.

Bibliography

Andrews, Kenneth R. "Ethics in Practice," *Harvard Business Review,* September 1989/October 1989: 99.

Aristotle. *The Basic Works of Aristotle,* ed. Richard McKeon (New York: Random House, 1941), *Politica,* translated by Benjamin Jowett.

Augustine, Norman R. "Reaping the returns of ethical acts: An American imperative," *Vital Speeches of the Day,* August 15, 1997: Vol. 63, No. 21: 658–660.

Badaracco, Joseph L., Jr., and Allen P. Web. "Business Ethics: A View from the Trenches," *California Management Review,* Winter 1995: 24.

Badaracco, Joseph L., Jr. *Defining Moments: When Managers Must Choose between Right and Right* (Boston: HBS Press, 1997).

Bellah, Robert N., Richard Madsen, William M. Sullivan, Ann Swidler, and Steven M. Tipton. *The Good Society* (New York: Alfred A. Knopf, 1991).

Bellah, Robert N., Richard Madsen, William M. Sullivan, Ann Swidler, and Steven M. Tipton. *Habits of the Heart: Individualism and Commitment in American Life* (New York, Harper-Perennial, 1985).

Blanton, Blanton. *Radical Honesty* (New York: Dell, 1996).

Bogan, Christopher E., and Michael J. English. *Benchmarking for Best Practices: Winning Through Innovative Adaptation* (New York: McGraw-Hill, 1994).

Bok, Sissela. *Lying: Moral Choice in Public and Private Life* (New York: Pantheon, 1978).

Bowie, Norman E. *Business Ethics: A Kantian Perspective* (Oxford: Blackwell Publishers, 1999).

Briskin, Alan. *The Stirring of Soul in the Workplace* (San Francisco: Berrett-Kohler, 1998).

Camenisch, Paul F. "A Religious Approach to Business Ethics," in *Perspectives in Business Ethics,* edited by Laura Pincus Hartman (Chicago: Irwin McGraw-Hill, 1998).

Carr, Alfred. "Is Business Bluffing Ethical?" *The New York Times,* March 9, 1967.

Carter, Stephen L. *Civility: Manners, Morals, and the Etiquette of Democracy* (New York: Basic Books, 1998).

Carter, Stephen L. *Integrity* (New York: HarperPerennial, 1996).

Case, John. *Open-Book Management* (New York: HarperBusiness, 1996).

Collins, James C., and Jerry I. Porras. *Built to Last: Successful Habits of Visionary Companies* (New York: HarperBusiness, 1994).

Daloz, Laurent A. Parks, Cheryl H. Keen, James P. Keen, and Sharon Daloz Parks. *Common Fire: Leading Lives of Commitment in a Complex World* (Boston: Beacon Press, 1996).

Davenport, Thomas O. *Human Capital: What It Is and Why People Invest It* (San Francisco: Jossey-Bass, 1999).

Drucker, Peter F. *Management Challenges for the 21st Century* (New York: HarperBusiness, 1999).

Elkington, John. *Cannibals with Forks: The Triple Bottom Line of 21st Century Business* (Stony Creek, Connecticut: New Society Publishers, 1998).

Friedman, Milton. "The Social Responsibility of a Business is to Increase Its Profits," *The New York Times Magazine,* September 3, 1970.

Gilligan, Carol. *In a Different Voice: Psychological Theory and Women's Development* (Cambridge, Massachusetts: Harvard University Press, 1982).

Goodpaster, Kenneth E. "Note on the Corporation as a Moral Environment," in *Ethics in Practice: Managing the Moral Corporation,* edited by Kenneth R. Andrews (Boston: HBS Press, 1989).

Hartman, Edwin. *Organizational Ethics and the Good Life* (New York: Oxford University Press, 1996).

Hawken, Paul. *The Ecology of Commerce* (New York: HarperBusiness, 1993).

Hoffman, W. Michael. "Business and Environmental Ethics," in *Perspectives in Business Ethics,* edited by Laura Pincus Hartman (Chicago: Irwin McGraw-Hill, 1998).

Howard, Philip K. *The Death of Common Sense: How Law Is Suffocating America* (New York: Random House, 1994).

James, William. *Pragmatism* (Indianapolis: Hackett Publishing Company, 1981).

Kanungo, Rabindra N., and Manuel Mendonca. *Ethical Dimensions of Leadership* (Thousand Oaks, California: Sage Publications, 1996).

Kidder, Rushworth M. *How Good People Make Tough Choices: Resolving the Dilemmas of Ethical Living* (New York: William Morrow, 1995).

Kotter, John P., and James L. Heskett. *Corporate Culture and Performance* (New York: The Free Press, 1992).

Lehmann, Paul. *Ethics in a Christian Context* (New York: Harper and Row, 1963).

Leopold, Aldo. *The Essential Aldo Leopold: Quotations and Commentaries,* edited by Curt Meine and Richard L. Knight (University of Wisconsin Press, 1999).

Lewicki, Roy J., and Robert J. Robinson. "Ethical and Unethical Bargaining Tactics: An Empirical Study," *Journal of Business Ethics,* 18: 211–228, 1998.

Maslow, Abraham H. with Deborah Stephens and Gary Heil. *Maslow on Management* (New York: John Wiley & Sons, 1998).

Morse, John. "The Missing Link between Virtue Theory and Business Ethics," *Journal of Applied Philosophy,* Vol. 16, No. 1, 1999: 51.

Murray, David. *Ethics in Organizations* (London: Kogan Page Limited, 1997).

Nash, Laura L. *Believers in Business* (Nashville: Thomas Nelson Publishers, 1994).

Nash, Laura L. "Ethics Without the Sermon," *Harvard Business Review,* November 1981/December 1981: 79.

Nash, Laura L. *Good Intentions Aside: A Manager's Guide to Resolving Ethical Problems* (Boston: HBS Press, 1990).

Olson, Walter K. *The Excuse Factory: How Employment Law is Paralyzing the American Workplace* (New York: The Free Press, 1997).

Parks, Sharon Daloz, Thomas R. Piper, and Mary C. Gentile. *Can Ethics Be Taught: Perspectives, Challenges, and Approaches at Harvard Business School* (Boston: HBS Press, 1993).

Peters, Tom, and Nancy Austin. *A Passion for Excellence: The Leadership Difference* (New York: Random House, 1985).

Solomon, Robert C. *Ethics and Excellence: Cooperation and Integrity in Business* (New York: Oxford University Press, 1993).

Solomon, Robert. "Is It Ever Right to Lie? (On Truth in Advertising)" in *Perspectives in Business Ethics,* edited by Laura Pincus Hartman (Chicago: Irwin McGraw-Hill, 1998).

Stackhouse, Max L. "The Ten Commandments: Economic Implications," in *On Moral Business: Classical and Contemporary Resources for Ethics in Economic Life,* edited by Max L. Stackhouse, Dennis P. McCann, and Shirley J. Roels with Preston Williams (Michigan: William B. Eerdmans, 1995).

Trevino, Linda Klebe, Gary R. Weaver, David G. Gibson, and Barbara Ley Toffler, "Managing Ethics and Legal Compliance: What Works and What Hurts," *California Management Review,* Winter 1999: 135.

Wheatley, Margaret J., and Myron Kellner-Rogers. *A Simpler Way* (San Francisco: Berrett-Kohler, 1999).

About the Author

Jeffrey L. Seglin is an editor-at-large at *Inc.* magazine where he writes a business ethics column called *Black & White*. For the 1998–1999 academic year, he was a fellow in residence at the Center for the Study of Values in Public Life at Harvard University. He writes the monthly "Right Thing" column on business and workplace ethics for the Sunday *New York Times*. And he is also an assistant professor in the graduate department of Writing, Literature, and Publishing at Emerson College.

At *Inc.*, he was founding editor for the launch of *Inc. Technology*, a quarterly management and technology magazine to which he contributes a column called "Road Warrior." He also served as the inaugural editor of the first two issues of "The State of Small Business," an annual publication from *Inc.* that explores the small business economy.

In addition to his work at *Inc.*, Seglin is the author and coauthor of more than a dozen books on small business, marketing, and banking. And he has written articles for a variety of publications.

He holds a master's degree in theology and literature from the Divinity School at Harvard University and an undergraduate degree in English from Bethany College in West Virginia. He has two grown children, both of whom are teachers. He lives in Boston with his wife, Nancy. Seglin can be contacted via e-mail at jseglin@post.harvard.edu.

Index